This

BLESSED PROMISES

from SCRIPTURE

is

Presented

To: _____

By: _____

Hilltop Baptist Church
4859 Route 286 Hwy W.
Indiana, PA 15701
www.myhilltop.org
HOPE FROM THE HILLTOP!

_____

Date: _____

BLESSED PROMISES from SCRIPTURE

ACKNOWLEDGEMENT

This book was compiled and prepared for publication by Missionaries Larry and Donna Stallings, with the desire that it will be a blessing and help to all who read it. God's Word will answer your questions and help solve your problems. Put your faith in the reality and truth of the Bible. It will never fail or disappoint you.

Scriptures quoted herein are from the
King James Version of the Bible.

ISBN 978-0-9837968-6-2

Published by:
Spread The Word Distributors
155 Whitman Hollow Road
Walhalla, SC 29691

larry.stallingsbps@att.net

PROFILE

As Larry traveled for the ministry, he noticed that when people got saved, most were given a Bible but they did not know where to turn to find help. In 1993, Larry and Donna saw a need they could fill and compiled "Blessed Promises from Scripture". There are over 1,000 verses from God's Word. It is easy to look in the topical reference and find "thus saith the Lord". Through this book, they have been able to touch the lives of tens of thousands of people here in America, as well as other English speaking countries.

SPECIAL THANKS

We would like to express a special **THANK YOU** to Maurice and Sandra Wells; our friends and co-laborers in Christ. We are truly grateful for your help in making this printed edition available.

Also, thank you to our friends and family, pastors, church members, our children, printing staff, co-workers, Pastor Bill Duttry, Dr. Charles Keen, Dr. Sam Caudill, and Pastor Ed Leake for their help and encouragement through the years.

TABLE OF CONTENTS

1. HELP FROM THE BIBLE

2. WHAT THE BIBLE SAYS ABOUT

3. THE BIBLE IS

4. BLESSINGS PROMISED TO BELIEVERS

5. THE BELIEVER IS

6. GOD'S GREAT COMMISSION

7. GOD'S GREAT SALVATION

HELP FROM
THE BIBLE . . .

When You Are Angry

For wrath killeth the foolish man, and envy slayeth the silly one.

JOB 5:2

He that is soon angry dealeth foolishly: and a man of wicked devices is hated.

He that is slow to wrath is of great understanding: but he that is hasty of spirit exalteth folly.

PROVERBS 14:17,29

A soft answer turneth away wrath: but grievous words stir up anger.

A wrathful man stirreth up strife: but he that is slow to anger appeaseth strife.

PROVERBS 15:1,18

He that is slow to anger is better than the mighty; and he that ruleth his spirit than he that taketh a city.

PROVERBS 16:32

Say not thou, I will recompense evil; but wait on the Lord, and he shall save thee.

PROVERBS 20:22

Make no friendship with an angry man; and with a furious man thou shalt not go:

Lest thou learn his ways, and get a snare to thy soul.

PROVERBS 22:24,25

He that hath no rule over his own spirit is like a city that is broken down, and without walls.

PROVERBS 25:28

An angry man stirreth up strife, and a furious man aboundeth in transgression.

PROVERBS 29:22

Be not hasty in thy spirit to be angry: for anger resteth in the bosom of fools.

ECCLESIASTES 7:9

But now ye also put off all these; anger, wrath, malice, blasphemy, filthy communication out of your mouth.

COLOSSIANS 3:8

Cease from anger, and forsake wrath: fret not thyself in any wise to do evil.

PSALM 37:8

Be ye angry, and sin not: let not the sun go down upon your wrath:

Let all bitterness, and wrath, and anger, and clamour, and evil speaking, be put away from you, with all malice:

And be ye kind one to another, tenderhearted, forgiving one another, even as God for Christ's sake hath forgiven you.

EPHESIANS 4:26,31,32

Judge not, and ye shall not be judged: condemn not, and ye shall not be condemned: forgive, and ye shall be forgiven:

LUKE 6:37

Blessed are the meek: for they shall inherit the earth.

But I say unto you, That whosoever is angry with his brother without a cause shall be in danger of the judgment: . . .

MATTHEW 5:5,22

Wherefore, my beloved brethren, let every man be swift to hear, slow to speak, slow to wrath:

For the wrath of man worketh not the righteousness of God.

JAMES 1:19,20

Dearly beloved, avenge not yourselves, but rather give place unto wrath: for it is written, Vengeance is mine; I will repay, saith the Lord.

ROMANS 12:19

With Covetousness

Incline my heart unto thy testimonies, and not to covetousness.

PSALM 119:36

. . . but he that hateth covetousness shall prolong his days.

PROVERBS 28:16

Shall not all these take up a parable against him, and a taunting proverb against him, and say, Woe to him that increaseth that which is not his! . . .

HABAKKUK 2:6

For what is a man profited, if he shall gain the whole world, and lose his own soul? or what shall a man give in exchange for his soul?

MATTHEW 16:26

But woe unto you that are rich! for ye have received your consolation.

LUKE 6:24

And he said unto them, Take heed, and beware of covetousness: for a man's life consisteth not in the abundance of the things which he possesseth.

LUKE 12:15

Labour not for the meat which perisheth, but for that meat which endureth unto everlasting life, which the Son of man shall give unto you: for him hath God the Father sealed.

JOHN 6:27

But fornication, and all uncleaness, or covetousness, let it not be once named among you, as becometh saints;

EPHESIANS 5:3

Mortify therefore your members which are upon the earth; fornication, uncleaness, inordinate affection, evil concupiscence, and covetousness, which is idolatry:

COLOSSIANS 3:5

For we brought nothing into this world, and it is certain we can carry nothing out.

I TIMOTHY 6:7

Let your conversation be without covetousness; and be content with such things as ye have: for he hath said, I will never leave thee, nor forsake thee.

HEBREWS 13:5

For Depression

Thou wilt shew me the path of life: in thy presence is fulness of joy; at thy right hand there are pleasures for evermore.

PSALM 16:11

The righteous cry, and the Lord heareth, and delivereth them out of all their troubles.

PSALM 34:17

Rest in the Lord, and wait patiently for him: fret not thyself because of him who prospereth in his way, because of the man who bringeth wicked devices to pass.

PSALM 37:7

Why art thou cast down, O my soul? and why art thou disquieted in me? hope thou in God: for I shall yet praise him for the help of his countenance.

PSALM 42:5

A merry heart maketh a cheerful countenance: but by sorrow of the heart the spirit is broken.

PROVERBS 15:13

The fear of the Lord tendeth to life: and he that hath it shall abide satisfied; he shall not be visited with evil.

PROVERBS 19:23

Better is an handful with quietness, than both the hands full with travail and vexation of spirit.

ECCLESIASTES 4:6

But straightway Jesus spake unto them, saying, Be of good cheer; it is I; be not afraid.

MATTHEW 14:27

If in this life only we have hope in Christ, we are of all men most miserable.

I CORINTHIANS 15:19

We are troubled on every side, yet not distressed; we are perplexed, but not in despair;

Persecuted, but not forsaken; cast down, but not destroyed;

II CORINTHIANS 4:8,9

Fear thou not; for I am with thee: be not dismayed; for I am thy God: I will strengthen thee; yea, I will help thee; yea, I will uphold thee with the right hand of my righteousness.

ISAIAH 41:10

For Direction In Life

. . . I will lead them in paths that they have not known: I will make darkness light before them, and crooked things straight. These things will I do unto them, and not forsake them.

ISAIAH 42:16

To give light to them that sit in darkness and in the shadow of death, to guide our feet into the way of peace.

LUKE 1:79

For this God is our God for ever and ever: he will be our guide even unto death.

PSALM 48:14

Thy word is a lamp unto my feet, and a light unto my path.

The entrance of thy words giveth light; it giveth understanding unto the simple.

Order my steps in thy word: and let not any iniquity have dominion over me.

PSALM 119:105,130,133

If I take the wings of the morning, and dwell in the uttermost parts of the sea;

Even there shall thy hand lead me, and thy right hand shall hold me.

PSALM 139:9,10

Man's goings are of the Lord; how can a man then understand his own way?

PROVERBS 20:24

The steps of a good man are ordered by the Lord: and he delighteth in his way.

PSALM 37:23

I will instruct thee and teach thee in the way which thou shalt go: I will guide thee with mine eye.

PSALM 32:8

The meek will he guide in judgment: and the meek will he teach his way.

PSALM 25:9

Thou shalt guide me with thy counsel, and afterward receive me to glory.

PSALM 73:24

He restoreth my soul: he leadeth me in the paths of righteousness for his name's sake.

PSALM 23:3

Howbeit when he, the Spirit of truth, is come, he will guide you into all truth: . . .

JOHN 16:13

He that walketh with wise men shall be wise: but a companion of fools shall be destroyed.

PROVERBS 13:20

Trust in the Lord with all thine heart; and lean not unto thine own understanding.

In all thy ways acknowledge him, and he shall direct thy paths.

PROVERBS 3:5,6

And thine ears shall hear a word behind thee, saying, This is the way, walk ye in it, when ye turn to the right hand, and when ye turn to the left.

ISAIAH 30:21

And the Lord shall guide thee continually, and satisfy thy soul in drought, and make fat thy bones: and thou shalt be like a watered garden, and like a spring of water, whose waters fail not.

ISAIAH 58:11

A man's heart deviseth his way: but the Lord directeth his steps.

PROVERBS 16:9

In Disappointments

Casting all your care upon him; for he careth for you.

I PETER 5:7

For his anger endureth but a moment; in his favour is life: weeping may endure for a night, but joy cometh in the morning.

PSALM 30:5

Why art thou cast down, O my soul? and why art thou disquieted within me? hope in God: for I shall yet praise him, who is the health of my countenance, and my God.

PSALM 43:5

Yea, though I walk through the valley of the shadow of death, I will fear no evil: for thou art with me; thy rod and thy staff they comfort me.

PSALM 23:4

The Lord is nigh unto them that are of a broken heart; and saveth such as be of a contrite spirit.

PSALM 34:18

In the day when I cried thou answeredst me, and strengthenedst me with strength in my soul.

PSALM 138:3

I know that the Lord will maintain the cause of the afflicted, and the right of the poor.

PSALM 140:12

He giveth power to the faint; and to them that have no might he increaseth strength.

ISAIAH 40:29

When thou passest through the waters, I will be with thee; and through the rivers, they shall not overflow thee: when thou walkest through the fire, thou shalt not be burned; neither shall the flame kindle upon thee.

ISAIAH 43:2

Sing, O heavens; and be joyful, O earth; and break forth into singing, O mountains: for the Lord hath comforted his people, and will have mercy upon his afflicted.

ISAIAH 49:13

I, even I, am he that comforteth you: . . .

ISAIAH 51:12

For I reckon that the sufferings of this present time are not worthy to be compared with the glory which shall be revealed in us.

For we are saved by hope: but hope that is seen is not hope: for what a man seeth, why doth he yet hope for?

And we know that all things work together for good to them that love God, to them who are the called according to his purpose.

ROMANS 8:18,24,28

The Lord is good, a strong hold in the day of trouble; and he knoweth them that trust in him.

NAHUM 1:7

Blessed are they that mourn: for they shall be comforted.

MATTHEW 5:4

But seek ye first the kingdom of God, and his righteousness; and all these things shall be added unto you.

MATTHEW 6:33

I will not leave you comfortless: I will come to you.

JOHN 14:18

In the multitude of my thoughts within me thy comforts delight my soul.

PSALM 94:19

This is my comfort in my affliction: for thy word hath quickened me.

PSALM 119:50

He healeth the broken in heart, and bindeth up their wounds.

PSALM 147:3

With Domestic Problems

Better is a dry morsel, and quietness therewith, than an house full of sacrifices with strife.

PROVERBS 17:1

A merry heart doeth good like a medicine: but a broken spirit drieth the bones.

PROVERBS 17:22

And I will betroth thee unto me for ever; yea, I will betroth thee unto me in righteousness, and in judgment, and in lovingkindness, and in mercies.

HOSEA 2:19

Let the husband render unto the wife due benevolence: and likewise also the wife unto the husband.

The wife hath not power of her own body, but the husband: and likewise also the husband hath not power of his own body, but the wife.

I CORINTHIANS 7:3,4

And now abideth faith, hope, charity, these three; but the greatest of these is charity.

I CORINTHIANS 13:13

Likewise, ye husbands, dwell with them according to knowledge, giving honour unto the wife, as unto the weaker vessel, and as being heirs together of the grace of life; that your prayers be not hindered.

I PETER 3:7

. . . but to the counsellors of peace is joy.

PROVERBS 12:20

Blessed are the peacemakers; for they shall be called the children of God.

MATTHEW 5:9

. . . Be perfect, be of good comfort, be of one mind, live in peace; and the God of love and peace shall be with you.

II CORINTHIANS 13:11

. . . If we love one another, God dwelleth in us, and his love is perfected in us.

I JOHN 4:12

And above all things have fervent charity among yourselves: for charity shall cover the multitude of sins.

I PETER 4:8

With Evil Thoughts

He that walketh uprightly walketh surely: but he that perverteth his ways shall be known.

PROVERBS 10:9

Commit thy works unto the Lord, and thy thoughts shall be established.

PROVERBS 16:3

Finally, brethren, whatsoever things are true, whatsoever things are honest, whatsoever things are just, whatsoever things are pure, whatsoever things are lovely, whatsoever things are of good report; if there be any virtue, and if there be any praise, think on these things.

PHILIPPIANS 4:8

Unto the pure all things are pure: but unto them that are defiled and unbelieving is nothing pure; but even their mind and conscience is defiled.

TITUS 1:15

Ye shall know them by their fruits. Do men gather grapes of thorns, or figs of thistles?

Wherefore by their fruits ye shall know them.

MATTHEW 7:16,20

Blessed are the pure in heart: for they shall see God.

MATTHEW 5:8

And he saith unto them, Are ye so without understanding also? Do ye not perceive, that whatsoever thing from without entereth into the man, it cannot defile him;

All these evil things come from within, and defile the man.

MARK 7:18,23

Let us draw near with a true heart in full assurance of faith, having our hearts sprinkled from an evil conscience, and our bodies washed with pure water.

HEBREWS 10:22

Let the wicked forsake his way, and the unrighteous man his thoughts: and let him return unto the Lord, and he will have mercy upon him; and to our God, for he will abundantly pardon.

ISAIAH 55:7

. . . Resist the devil, and he will flee from you.

JAMES 4:7

. . . And if any man sin, we have an advocate with the Father, Jesus Christ the righteous:

I JOHN 2:1

Ye are of God, little children, and have overcome them: because greater is he that is in you, than he that is in the world.

I JOHN 4:4

. . . for I will forgive their iniquity, and I will remember their sin no more.

JEREMIAH 31:34

When Experiencing Fear

I sought the Lord, and he heard me, and delivered me from all my fears.

PSALM 34:4

And Moses said unto the people, Fear ye not, stand still, and see the salvation of the Lord, which he will shew to you to-day: . . .

EXODUS 14:13

Behold, God is my salvation; I will trust, and not be afraid: for the Lord JEHOVAH is my strength and my song; he also is become my salvation.

ISAIAH 12:2

Fear thou not; for I am with thee: be not dismayed; for I am thy God: I will strengthen thee; yea, I will help thee; yea, I will uphold thee with the right hand of my righteousness.

ISAIAH 41:10

Take therefore no thought for the morrow: for the morrow shall take thought for the things of itself. Sufficient unto the day is the evil thereof.

MATTHEW 6:34

For ye have not received the spirit of bondage again to fear; but ye have received the Spirit of adoption, whereby we cry, Abba, Father.

ROMANS 8:15

For God hath not given us the spirit of fear; but of power, and of love, and of a sound mind.

II TIMOTHY 1:7

So that we may boldly say, The Lord is my helper, and I will not fear what man shall do unto me.

HEBREWS 13:6

There is no fear in love; but perfect love casteth out fear: because fear hath torment. He that feareth is not made perfect in love.

I JOHN 4:18

In God have I put my trust: I will not be afraid what man can do unto me.

PSALM 56:11

What shall we then say to these things? If God be for us, who can be against us?

Nay, in all these things we are more than conquerors through him that loved us.

ROMANS 8:31,37

Be of good courage, and he shall strengthen your heart, all ye that hope in the Lord.

PSALM 31:24

Peace I leave with you, my peace I give unto you: not as the world giveth, give I unto you. Let not your heart be troubled, neither let it be afraid.

JOHN 14:27

And fear not them which kill the body, but are not able to kill the soul: but rather fear him which is able to destroy both soul and body in hell.

MATTHEW 10:28

Rejoice in the Lord alway: and again I say, Rejoice.

Let your moderation be known unto all men. The Lord is at hand.

Be careful for nothing; but in every thing by prayer and supplication with thanksgiving let your requests be made known unto God.

And the peace of God, which passeth all understanding, shall keep your hearts and minds through Christ Jesus.

PHILIPPIANS 4:4,5,6,7

In Financial Difficulties

The Lord maketh poor, and maketh rich: he bringeth low, and lifteth up.

He raiseth up the poor out of the dust, and lifteth up the beggar from the dunghill, to set them among princes, and to make them inherit the throne of glory: for the pillars of the earth are the Lord's, and he hath set the world upon them.

I SAMUEL 2:7,8

Riches profit not in the day of wrath: but righteousness delivereth from death.

PROVERBS 11:4

There is that maketh himself rich, yet hath nothing: there is that maketh himself poor, yet hath great riches.

PROVERBS 13:7

The rich and poor meet together: the Lord is the maker of them all.

The rich ruleth over the poor, and the borrower is servant to the lender.

PROVERBS 22:2,7

For there is no difference between the Jew and the Greek: for the same Lord over all is rich unto all that call upon him.

ROMANS 10:12

And the cares of this world, and the deceitfulness of riches, and the lusts of other things entering in, choke the word, and it becometh unfruitful.

MARK 4:19

I have been young, and now am old; yet have I not seen the righteous forsaken, nor his seed begging bread.

PSALM 37:25

As he came forth of his mother's womb, naked shall he return to go as he came, and shall take nothing of his labour, which he may carry away in his hand.

ECCLESIASTES 5:15

Thus saith the Lord, Let not the wise man glory in his wisdom, neither let the mighty man glory in his might, let not the rich man glory in his riches:

But let him that glorieth glory in this, that he understandeth and knoweth me, that I am the Lord which exercise lovingkindness, judgment, and righteousness, in the earth: for in these things I delight, saith the Lord.

JEREMIAH 9:23,24

For the love of money is the root of all evil: which while some coveted after, they have erred from the faith, and pierced themselves through with many sorrows.

I TIMOTHY 6:10

Lay not up for yourselves treasures upon earth, where moth and rust doth corrupt, and where thieves break through and steal:

But lay up for yourselves treasures in heaven, where neither moth nor rust doth corrupt, and where thieves do not break through nor steal:

For where your treasure is, there will your heart be also.

MATTHEW 6:19,20,21

For all these things do the nations of the world seek after: and your Father knoweth that ye have need of these things.

But rather seek ye the kingdom of God; and all these things shall be added unto you.

LUKE 12:30,31

But my God shall supply all your need according to his riches in glory by Christ Jesus.

PHILIPPIANS 4:19

. . . and as long as he sought the Lord, God made him to prosper.

II CHRONICLES 26:5

Blessed be the Lord, who daily loadeth us with benefits, even the God of our salvation. Selah.

PSALM 68:19

For the Lord God is a sun and shield: the Lord will give grace and glory: no good thing will he withhold from them that walk uprightly.

PSALM 84:11

For Impatience

It is good that a man should both hope and quietly wait for the salvation of the Lord.

LAMENTATIONS 3:26

Let integrity and uprightness preserve me; for I wait on thee.

PSALM 25:21

Wait on the Lord: be of good courage, and he shall strengthen thine heart: wait, I say, on the Lord.

PSALM 27:14

I waited patiently for the Lord; and he inclined unto me, and heard my cry.

PSALM 40:1

I wait for the Lord, my soul doth wait, and in his word do I hope.

PSALM 130:5

The thoughts of the diligent tend only to plenteousness; but of every one that is hasty only to want.

PROVERBS 21:5

If a man die, shall he live again? all the days of my appointed time will I wait, till my change come.

JOB 14:14

But they that wait upon the Lord shall renew their strength; they shall mount up with wings as eagles; they shall run, and not be weary; and they shall walk, and not faint.

ISAIAH 40:31

But that on the good ground are they, which in an honest and good heart, having heard the word, keep it, and bring forth fruit with patience.

LUKE 8:15

And not only so, but we glory in tribulations also: knowing that tribulation worketh patience;

And patience, experience; and experience, hope.

ROMANS 5:3,4

But if we hope for that we see not, then do we with patience wait for it.

ROMANS 8:25

For whatsoever things were written aforetime were written for our learning, that we through patience and comfort of the scriptures might have hope.

ROMANS 15:4

And let us not be weary in welldoing: for in due season we shall reap, if we faint not.

GALATIANS 6:9

For ye have need of patience, that, after ye have done the will of God, ye might receive the promise.

HEBREWS 10:36

Knowing this, that the trying of your faith worketh patience.

But let patience have her perfect work, that ye may be perfect and entire, wanting nothing.

JAMES 1:3,4

Behold, we count them happy which endure. Ye have heard of the patience of Job, and have seen the end of the Lord; that the Lord is very pitiful, and of tender mercy.

JAMES 5:11

Wherefore seeing we also are compassed about with so great a cloud of witnesses, let us lay aside every weight, and the sin which doth so easily beset us, and let us run with patience the race that is set before us.

HEBREWS 12:1

To every thing there is a season, and a time to every purpose under the heaven:

ECCLESIASTES 3:1

Better is the end of a thing than the beginning thereof: and the patient in spirit is better than the proud in spirit.

ECCLESIASTES 7:8

When Given To Jealousy

Fret not thyself because of evildoers, neither be thou envious against the workers of iniquity.

PSALM 37:1

Let us walk honestly, as in the day; not in rioting and drunkenness, not in chambering and wantonness, not in strife and envying.

ROMANS 13:13

Be not thou afraid when one is made rich, when the glory of his house is increased;

For when he dieth he shall carry nothing away: his glory shall not descend after him.

PSALM 49:16,17

Wrath is cruel, and anger is outrageous; but who is able to stand before envy?

PROVERBS 27:4

Set me as a seal upon thine heart, as a seal upon thine arm: for love is strong as death; jealousy is cruel as the grave: the coals thereof are coals of fire, which hath a most vehement flame.

SONG OF SOLOMON 8:6

Charity suffereth long, and is kind; charity envieth not; charity vaunteth not itself, is not puffed up,

I CORINTHIANS 13:4

Let us not be desirous of vain glory, provoking one another, envying one another.

GALATIANS 5:26

For where envying and strife is, there is confusion and every evil work.

JAMES 3:16

Be not overcome of evil, but overcome evil with good.

ROMANS 12:21

During The Loss Of Loved Ones

But I would not have you to be ignorant, brethren, concerning them which are asleep, that ye sorrow not, even as others which have no hope.

I THESSALONIANS 4:13

Cast thy burden upon the Lord, and he shall sustain thee: he shall never suffer the righteous to be moved.

PSALM 55:22

Thy sun shall no more go down; neither shall thy moon withdraw itself: for the Lord shall be thine everlasting light, and the days of thy mourning shall be ended.

ISAIAH 60:20

Verily, verily, I say unto you, That ye shall weep and lament, but the world shall rejoice: and ye shall be sorrowful, but your sorrow shall be turned into joy.

JOHN 16:20

Blessed are ye that hunger now: for ye shall be filled. Blessed are ye that weep now: for ye shall laugh.

LUKE 6:21

He will swallow up death in victory; and the Lord God will wipe away tears from off all faces; and the rebuke of his people shall he take away from off all the earth: for the Lord hath spoken it.

ISAIAH 25:8

For the people shall dwell in Zion at Jerusalem: thou shalt weep no more: he will be very gracious unto thee at the voice of thy cry; when he shall hear it, he will answer thee.

ISAIAH 30:19

O death, where is thy sting? O grave, where is thy victory?

But thanks be to God, which giveth us the victory through our Lord Jesus Christ.

I CORINTHIANS 15:55,57

Let not your heart be troubled: ye believe in God, believe also in me.

In my Father's house are many mansions: if it were not so, I would have told you. I go to prepare a place for you.

And if I go and prepare a place for you, I will come again, and receive you unto myself; that where I am, there ye may be also.

JOHN 14:1,2,3

The Lord is my shepherd; I shall not want.

He maketh me to lie down in green pastures: he leadeth me beside the still waters.

He restoreth my soul: he leadeth me in the paths of righteousness for his name's sake.

Yea, though I walk through the valley of the shadow of death, I will fear no evil: for thou art with me; thy rod and thy staff they comfort me.

Thou preparest a table before me in the presence of mine enemies: thou anointest my head with oil; my cup runneth over.

Surely goodness and mercy shall follow me all the days of my life: and I will dwell in the house of the Lord for ever.

PSALM 23

With Moral Weakness

The Lord God is my strength, and he will make my feet like hinds' feet, and he will make me to walk upon mine high places. . . .

HABAKKUK 3:19

Jesus said unto him, If thou canst believe, all things are possible to him that believeth.

MARK 9:23

Watch ye, stand fast in the faith, quit you like men, be strong.

I CORINTHIANS 16:13

I can do all things through Christ which strengtheneth me.

PHILIPPIANS 4:13

Nay, in all these things we are more than conquerors through him that loved us.

ROMANS 8:37

For we have not an high priest which cannot be touched with the feeling of our infirmities; but was in all points tempted like as we are, yet without sin.

HEBREWS 4:15

Say to them that are of a fearful heart, Be strong, fear not: behold, your God will come with vengeance, even God with a recompence; he will come and save you.

ISAIAH 35:4

With Injured Pride

Surely he scorneth the scorners: but he giveth grace unto the lowly.

PROVERBS 3:34

Pride goeth before destruction, and an haughty spirit before a fall.

PROVERBS 16:18

Talk no more so exceeding proudly; let not arrogancy come out of your mouth: for the Lord is a God of knowledge, and by him actions are weighed.

I SAMUEL 2:3

And whosoever shall exalt himself shall be abased; and he that shall humble himself shall be exalted.

MATTHEW 23:12

For who maketh thee to differ from another? and what hast thou that thou didst not receive? now if thou didst receive it, why dost thou glory, as if thou hadst not received it?

I CORINTHIANS 4:7

For what glory is it, if, when ye be buffeted for your faults, ye shall take it patiently? but if, when ye do well, and suffer for it, ye take it patiently, this is acceptable with God.

I PETER 2:20

When pride cometh, then cometh shame: but with the lowly is wisdom.

PROVERBS 11:2

An high look, and a proud heart, and the plowing of the wicked, is sin.

PROVERBS 21:4

He that is of a proud heart stirreth up strife: but he that putteth his trust in the Lord shall be made fat.

He that trusteth in his own heart is a fool: but whoso walketh wisely, he shall be delivered.

PROVERBS 28:25,26

During Personal Sorrow

Depart from me, all ye workers of iniquity; for the Lord hath heard the voice of my weeping.

PSALM 6:8

The Lord is nigh unto them that are of a broken heart; and saveth such as be of a contrite spirit.

PSALM 34:18

I have been young, and now am old; yet have I not seen the righteous forsaken, nor his seed begging bread.

PSALM 37:25

Why art thou cast down, O my soul? and why art thou disquieted within me? hope in God: for I shall yet praise him, who is the health of my countenance, and my God.

PSALM 43:5

The sacrifices of God are a broken spirit: a broken and a contrite heart, O God, thou wilt not despise.

PSALM 51:17

He healeth the broken in heart, and bindeth up their wounds.

PSALM 147:3

When my father and my mother forsake me, then the Lord will take me up.

PSALM 27:10

Blessed are they that mourn: for they shall be comforted.

The eternal God is thy refuge, and underneath are the everlasting arms: and he shall thrust out the enemy from before thee; and shall say, Destroy them.

Sing, O heavens; and be joyful, O earth; and break forth into singing, O mountains: for the Lord hath comforted his people, and will have mercy upon his afflicted.

Can a woman forget her sucking child, that she should not have compassion on the son of her womb? yea, they may forget, yet will I not forget thee.

Behold, I have graven thee upon the palms of my hands; thy walls are continually before me.

Come unto me, all ye that labour and are heavy laden, and I will give you rest.

Teaching them to observe all things whatsoever I have commanded you: and, lo, I am with you alway, even unto the end of the world. Amen.

I am come a light into the world, that whosoever believeth on me should not abide in darkness.

JOHN 12:46

If we suffer, we shall also reign with him: . . .

II TIMOTHY 2:12

Sorrow is better than laughter: for by the sadness of the countenance the heart is made better.

ECCLESIASTES 7:3

. . . but if, when ye do well, and suffer for it, ye take it patiently, this is acceptable with God.

I PETER 2:20

He that overcometh shall inherit all things; and I will be his God, and he shall be my son.

REVELATION 21:7

Casting all your care upon him; for he careth for you.

I PETER 5:7

During Times Of Temptation

There hath no temptation taken you but such as is common to man: but God is faithful, who will not suffer you to be tempted above that ye are able; but will with the temptation also make a way to escape, that ye may be able to bear it.

I CORINTHIANS 10:13

And lead us not into temptation, but deliver us from evil: For thine is the kingdom, and the power, and the glory, for ever. Amen.

MATTHEW 6:13

Watch and pray, that ye enter not into temptation: the spirit indeed is willing, but the flesh is weak.

MATTHEW 26:41

Put on the whole armour of God, that ye may be able to stand against the wiles of the devil.

EPHESIANS 6:11

Be sober, be vigilant; because your adversary the devil, as a roaring lion, walketh about, seeking whom he may devour.

I PETER 5:8

The Lord knoweth how to deliver the godly out of temptations, and to reserve the unjust unto the day of judgment to be punished.

II PETER 2:9

Blessed is the man that endureth temptation: for when he is tried, he shall receive the crown of life, which the Lord hath promised to them that love him.

Let no man say when he is tempted, I am tempted of God: for God cannot be tempted with evil, neither tempteth he any man:

But every man is tempted, when he is drawn away of his own lust, and enticed.

JAMES 1:12,13,14

Ye therefore, beloved, seeing ye know these things before, beware lest ye also, being led away with the error of the wicked, fall from your own steadfastness.

II PETER 3:17

Because thou hast kept the word of my patience, I also will keep thee from the hour of temptation, which shall come upon all the world, to try them that dwell upon the earth.

REVELATION 3:10

For sin shall not have dominion over you: for ye are not under the law, but under grace.

ROMANS 6:14

Nay, in all these things we are more than conquerors through him that loved us.

ROMANS 8:37

Be not overcome of evil, but overcome evil with good.

ROMANS 12:21

For in that he himself hath suffered being tempted, he is able to succour them that are tempted.

HEBREWS 2:18

. . . Resist the devil, and he will flee from you.

JAMES 4:7

These things I have spoken unto you, that in me ye might have peace. In the world ye shall have tribulation: but be of good cheer; I have overcome the world.

JOHN 16:33

Ye are of God, little children, and have overcome them: because greater is he that is in you, than he that is in the world.

I JOHN 4:4

In Time Of Trouble

The Lord is my light and my salvation; whom shall I fear? the Lord is the strength of my life; of whom shall I be afraid?

PSALM 27:1

God is our refuge and strength, a very present help in trouble.

PSALM 46:1

Remember the word unto thy servant, upon which thou hast caused me to hope.

PSALM 119:49

The Lord also will be a refuge for the oppressed, a refuge in times of trouble.

PSALM 9:9

For in the time of trouble he shall hide me in his pavilion: in the secret of his tabernacle shall he hide me; he shall set me up upon a rock.

PSALM 27:5

I will be glad and rejoice in thy mercy: for thou hast considered my trouble; thou hast known my soul in adversities;

PSALM 31:7

And call upon me in the day of trouble: I will deliver thee, and thou shalt glorify me.

PSALM 50:15

He shall call upon me, and I will answer him: I will be with him in trouble; I will deliver him, and honour him.

PSALM 91:15

Though I walk in the midst of trouble, thou wilt revive me: thou shalt stretch forth thine hand against the wrath of mine enemies, and thy right hand shall save me.

PSALM 138:7

I will lift up mine eyes unto the hills, from whence cometh my help.

My help cometh from the Lord, which made heaven and earth.

PSALM 121:1,2

I will not leave you comfortless: I will come to you.

Peace I leave with you, my peace I give unto you: not as the world giveth, give I unto you. Let not your heart be troubled, neither let it be afraid.

JOHN 14:18,27

Blessed be God, even the Father of our Lord Jesus Christ, the Father of mercies, and the God of all comfort;

Who comforteth us in all our tribulation, that we may be able to comfort them which are in any trouble, by the comfort wherewith we ourselves are comforted of God.

II CORINTHIANS 1:3,4

As one whom his mother comforteth, so will I comfort you; and ye shall be comforted in Jerusalem.

ISAIAH 66:13

When thou passest through the waters, I will be with thee; and through the rivers, they shall not overflow thee: when thou walkest through the fire, thou shalt not be burned; neither shall the flame kindle upon thee.

ISAIAH 43:2

The righteous is delivered out of trouble, and the wicked cometh in his stead.

PROVERBS 11:8

The Lord is good, a strong hold in the day of trouble; and he knoweth them that trust in him.

NAHUM 1:7

And we know that all things work together for good to them that love God, to them who are the called according to his purpose.

ROMANS 8:28

Casting all your care upon him; for he careth for you.

I PETER 5:7

When You Need Wisdom

The fear of the Lord is the beginning of wisdom: and the knowledge of the holy is understanding.

PROVERBS 9:10

He that getteth wisdom loveth his own soul: he that keepeth understanding shall find good.

PROVERBS 19:8

Understanding is a wellspring of life unto him that hath it: but the instruction of fools is folly.

PROVERBS 16:22

But the natural man receiveth not the things of the Spirit of God: for they are foolishness unto him: neither can he know them, because they are spiritually discerned.

I CORINTHIANS 2:14

And we know that the Son of God is come, and hath given us an understanding, that we may know him that is true, and we are in him that is true, even in his Son Jesus Christ. This is the true God, and eternal life.

I JOHN 5:20

I will bless the Lord, who hath given me counsel: my reins also instruct me in the night seasons.

PSALM 16:7

Evil men understand not judgment: but they that seek the Lord understand all things.

PROVERBS 28:5

For God giveth to a man that is good in his sight wisdom, and knowledge, and joy: but to the sinner he giveth travail, to gather and to heap up, that he may give to him that is good before God. This also is vanity and vexation of spirit.

ECCLESIASTES 2:26

If any of you lack wisdom, let him ask of God, that giveth to all men liberally, and upbraideth not; and it shall be given him.

JAMES 1:5

He restoreth my soul: he leadeth me in the paths of righteousness for his name's sake.

PSALM 23:3

And the Lord shall guide thee continually, and satisfy thy soul in drought, and make fat thy bones: and thou shalt be like a watered garden, and like a spring of water, whose waters fail not.

ISAIAH 58:11

Thou shalt guide me with thy counsel, and afterward receive me to glory.

PSALM 73:24

And thine ears shall hear a word behind thee, saying, This is the way, walk ye in it, when ye turn to the right hand, and when ye turn to the left.

ISAIAH 30:21

Behold, thou desirest truth in the inward parts: and in the hidden part thou shalt make me to know wisdom.

PSALM 51:6

For the Lord giveth wisdom: out of his mouth cometh knowledge and understanding.

He layeth up sound wisdom for the righteous: he is a buckler to them that walk uprightly.

PROVERBS 2:6,7

Then shall we know, if we follow on to know the Lord: . . .

HOSEA 6:3

For God, who commanded the light to shine out of darkness, hath shined in our hearts, to give the light of the knowledge of the glory of God in the face of Jesus Christ.

II CORINTHIANS 4:6

Wisdom is the principal thing; therefore get wisdom: and with all thy getting get understanding.

PROVERBS 4:7

A wise man will hear, and will increase learning; and a man of understanding shall attain unto wise counsels:

The fear of the Lord is the beginning of knowledge: but fools despise wisdom and instruction.

PROVERBS 1:5,7

Trust in the Lord with all thine heart; and lean not unto thine own understanding.

In all thy ways acknowledge him, and he shall direct thy paths.

PROVERBS 3:5,6

Happy is the man that findeth wisdom, and the man that getteth understanding.

For the merchandise of it is better than the merchandise of silver, and the gain thereof than fine gold.

PROVERBS 3:13,14

WHAT THE
BIBLE SAYS
ABOUT . . .

The Bible

Great peace have they which love thy law: and nothing shall offend them.

PSALM 119:165

Thy word is a lamp unto my feet, and a light unto my path.

PSALM 119:105

Heaven and earth shall pass away, but my words shall not pass away.

MATTHEW 24:35

Search the scriptures; for in them ye think ye have eternal life . . .

JOHN 5:39

And take the helmet of salvation, and the sword of the Spirit, which is the word of God:

EPHESIANS 6:17

For I am not ashamed of the gospel of Christ: for it is the power of God unto salvation to every one that believeth; to the Jew first, and also to the Greek.

ROMANS 1:16

For the word of God is quick, and powerful, and sharper than any two-edged sword, piercing even to the dividing asunder of soul and spirit, and of the joints, and marrow, and is a discerner of the thoughts and intents of the heart.

HEBREWS 4:12

The law of the Lord is perfect, converting the soul: the testimony of the Lord is sure, making wise the simple.

The statutes of the Lord are right, rejoicing the heart: the commandment of the Lord is pure, enlightening the eyes.

PSALM 19:7,8

For the commandment is a lamp; and the law is light; and reproofs of instruction are the way of life:

PROVERBS 6:23

The grass withereth, the flower fadeth: but the word of our God shall stand for ever.

ISAIAH 40:8

All scripture is given by inspiration of God, and is profitable for doctrine, for reproof, for correction, for instruction in righteousness:

II TIMOTHY 3:16

Blessed is he that readeth, and they that hear the words of this prophecy, and keep those things which are written therein: . . .

REVELATION 1:3

The Blood

And the blood shall be to you for a token upon the houses where ye are: and when I see the blood, I will pass over you, and the plague shall not be upon you to destroy you, when I smite the land of Egypt.

EXODUS 12:13

When I say unto the wicked, Thou shalt surely die; and thou givest him not warning, nor speakest to warn the wicked from his wicked way, to save his life; the same wicked man shall die in his iniquity; but his blood will I require at thine hand.

EZEKIEL 3:18

And he said unto them, This is my blood of the new testament, which is shed for many.

MARK 14:24

And he took bread, and gave thanks, and brake it, and gave unto them, saying, This is my body which is given for you: this do in remembrance of me.

Likewise also the cup after supper, saying, This cup is the new testament in my blood, which is shed for you.

LUKE 22:19,20

Take heed therefore unto yourselves, and to all the flock, over the which the Holy Ghost hath made you overseers, to feed the church of God, which he hath purchased with his own blood.

ACTS 20:28

Whom God hath set forth to be a propitiation through faith in his blood, to declare his righteousness for the remission of sins that are past, through the forbearance of God;

ROMANS 3:25

In whom we have redemption through his blood, the forgiveness of sins, according to the riches of his grace;

EPHESIANS 1:7

Neither by the blood of goats and calves, but by his own blood he entered in once into the holy place, having obtained eternal redemption for us.

For if the blood of bulls and of goats, and the ashes of an heifer sprinkling the unclean, sanctifieth to the purifying of the flesh:

How much more shall the blood of Christ, who through the eternal Spirit offered himself without spot to God, purge your conscience from dead works to serve the living God?

And almost all things are by the law purged with blood; and without shedding of blood is no remission.

HEBREWS 9:12,13,14,22

For the bodies of those beasts, whose blood is brought into the sanctuary by the high priest for sin, are burned without the camp.

Wherefore Jesus also, that he might sanctify the people with his own blood, suffered without the gate.

Let us go forth therefore unto him without the camp, bearing his reproach.

HEBREWS 13:11,12,13

Forasmuch as ye know that ye were not redeemed with corruptible things, as silver and gold, from your vain conversation received by tradition from your fathers;

But with the precious blood of Christ, as of a lamb without blemish and without spot:

I PETER 1:18,19

But if we walk in the light, as he is in the light, we have fellowship one with another, and the blood of Jesus Christ his Son cleanseth us from all sin.

I JOHN 1:7

And from Jesus Christ, who is the faithful witness, and the first begotten of the dead, and the prince of the kings of the earth. Unto him that loved us, and washed us from our sins in his own blood,

And hath made us kings and priests unto God and his Father; to him be glory and dominion for ever and ever. Amen.

REVELATION 1:5,6

Business Matters

He that is surety for a stranger shall smart for it: and he that hateth suretyship is sure.

PROVERBS 11:15

A wicked man taketh a gift out of the bosom to pervert the ways of judgment.

PROVERBS 17:23

Be thou diligent to know the state of thy flocks, and look well to thy herds.

For riches are not for ever: and doth the crown endure to every generation?

PROVERBS 27:23,24

A false balance is abomination to the Lord: but a just weight is his delight.

PROVERBS 11:1

Withhold not good from them to whom it is due, when it is in the power of thine hand to do it.

PROVERBS 3:27

The Lord will not suffer the souls of the righteous to famish: but he casteth away the substance of the wicked.

He becometh poor that dealeth with a slack hand: but the hand of the diligent maketh rich.

PROVERBS 10:3,4

If they obey and serve him, they shall spend their days in prosperity, and their years in pleasures.

JOB 36:11

The liberal soul shall be made fat: and he that watereth shall be watered also himself.

He that trusteth in his riches shall fall: but the righteous shall flourish as a branch.

PROVERBS 11:25,28

Prepare thy work without, and make it fit for thyself in the field; and afterwards build thine house.

PROVERBS 24:27

But seek ye first the kingdom of God, and his righteousness; and all these things shall be added unto you.

MATTHEW 6:33

Not slothful in business; fervent in spirit; serving the Lord;

ROMANS 12:11

Death

And as it is appointed unto men once to die, but after this the judgment:

HEBREWS 9:27

Yea, though I walk through the valley of the shadow of death, I will fear no evil: for thou art with me; thy rod and thy staff they comfort me.

PSALM 23:4

For this God is our God for ever and ever: he will be our guide even unto death.

PSALM 48:14

For thou hast delivered my soul from death: wilt not thou deliver my feet from falling, that I may walk before God in the light of the living?

PSALM 56:13

Precious in the sight of the Lord is the death of his saints.

PSALM 116:15

He will swallow up death in victory; and the Lord God will wipe away tears from off all faces; . . .

ISAIAH 25:8

What man is he that liveth, and shall not see death? shall he deliver his soul from the hand of the grave? Selah.

PSALM 89:48

The days of our years are threescore years and ten; and if by reason of strength they be fourscore years, yet is their strength labour and sorrow; for it is soon cut off, and we fly away.

So teach us to number our days, that we may apply our hearts unto wisdom.

PSALM 90:10,12

Verily, verily, I say unto you, If a man keep my saying, he shall never see death.

JOHN 8:51

O death, where is thy sting? O grave, where is thy victory?

I CORINTHIANS 15:55

But God will redeem my soul from the power of the grave: for he shall receive me. Selah.

PSALM 49:15

. . . but though our outward man perish, yet the inward man is renewed day by day.

II CORINTHIANS 4:16

For I am persuaded, that neither death, nor life, nor angels, nor principalities, nor powers, nor things present, nor things to come,

Nor height, nor depth, nor any other creature, shall be able to separate us from the love of God, which is in Christ Jesus our Lord.

ROMANS 8:38,39

Deliverance

And call upon me in the day of trouble: I will
deliver thee, and thou shalt glorify me.

PSALM 50:15

For he hath delivered me out of all trouble:
and mine eye hath seen his desire upon mine
enemies.

PSALM 54:7

For thou hast delivered my soul from death:
wilt not thou deliver my feet from falling, that
I may walk before God in the light of the living?

PSALM 56:13

Deliver me from mine enemies, O my God:
defend me from them that rise up against me.

PSALM 59:1

Deliver me out of the mire, and let me not sink:
let me be delivered from them that hate me,
and out of the deep waters.

PSALM 69:14

Deliver me in thy righteousness, and cause me
to escape: incline thine ear unto me, and save
me.

PSALM 71:2

For he shall deliver the needy when he crieth;
the poor also, and him that hath no helper.

PSALM 72:12

For thou hast delivered my soul from death, mine eyes from tears, and my feet from falling.

PSALM 116:8

The Lord is on my side; I will not fear: what can man do unto me?

PSALM 118:6

Though I walk in the midst of trouble, thou wilt revive me: thou shalt stretch forth thine hand against the wrath of mine enemies, and thy right hand shall save me.

PSALM 138:7

Now unto him that is able to keep you from falling, and to present you faultless before the presence of his glory with exceeding joy,

JUDE 24

The Devil

Be sober, be vigilant; because your adversary the devil, as a roaring lion, walketh about, seeking whom he may devour:

Whom resist stedfast in the faith, knowing that the same afflictions are accomplished in your brethren that are in the world.

I PETER 5:8,9

Neither give place to the devil.

EPHESIANS 4:27

Put on the whole armour of God, that ye may be able to stand against the wiles of the devil.

EPHESIANS 6:11

Submit yourselves therefore to God. Resist the devil, and he will flee from you.

JAMES 4:7

He that committeth sin is of the devil; for the devil sinneth from the beginning. For this purpose the Son of God was manifested, that he might destroy the works of the devil.

I JOHN 3:8

And he laid hold on the dragon, that old serpent, which is the Devil, and Satan, and bound him a thousand years.

REVELATION 20:2

How art thou fallen from heaven, O Lucifer, son of the morning! how art thou cut down to the ground, which didst weaken the nations!

For thou hast said in thine heart, I will ascend into heaven, I will exalt my throne above the stars of God: I will sit also upon the mount of the congregation, in the sides of the north:

I will ascend above the heights of the clouds; I will be like the most High.

Yet thou shalt be brought down to hell, to the sides of the pit.

ISAIAH 14:12,13,14,15

Eternal Life

Then Simon Peter answered him, Lord, to whom shall we go? thou hast the words of eternal life.

JOHN 6:68

And I give unto them eternal life; and they shall never perish, neither shall any man pluck them out of my hand.

JOHN 10:28

But he shall receive an hundredfold now in this time, houses, and brethren, and sisters, and mothers, and children, and lands, with persecutions; and in the world to come eternal life.

MARK 10:30

To them who by patient continuance in well-doing seek for glory and honour and immortality, eternal life:

ROMANS 2:7

For the wages of sin is death; but the gift of God is eternal life through Jesus Christ our Lord.

ROMANS 6:23

And this is the promise that he hath promised us, even eternal life.

I JOHN 2:25

And this is the record, that God hath given to us eternal life, and this life is in his Son.

These things have I written unto you that believe on the name of the Son of God; that ye may know that ye have eternal life, and that ye may believe on the name of the Son of God.

I JOHN 5:11,13

Jesus said unto her, I am the resurrection, and the life: he that believeth in me, though he were dead, yet shall he live:

And whosoever liveth and believeth in me shall never die. Believest thou this?

JOHN 11:25,26

For since by man came death, by man came also the resurrection of the dead.

I CORINTHIANS 15:21

And God shall wipe away all tears from their eyes; and there shall be no more death, neither sorrow, nor crying, neither shall there be any more pain: for the former things are passed away.

REVELATION 21:4

Faith

Now faith is the substance of things hoped for, the evidence of things not seen.

HEBREWS 11:1

That ye be not slothful, but followers of them who through faith and patience inherit the promises.

HEBREWS 6:12

For I say, through the grace given unto me, to every man that is among you, not to think of himself more highly than he ought to think; but to think soberly, according as God hath dealt to every man the measure of faith.

ROMANS 12:3

Therefore being justified by faith, we have peace with God through our Lord Jesus Christ.

ROMANS 5:1

So then faith cometh by hearing, and hearing by the word of God.

ROMANS 10:17

Now the just shall live by faith: . . .

HEBREWS 10:38

For ye are all the children of God by faith in Christ Jesus.

GALATIANS 3:26

For by grace are ye saved through faith; and that not of yourselves: it is the gift of God:

EPHESIANS 2:8

Watch ye, stand fast in the faith, quit you like men, be strong.

I CORINTHIANS 16:13

But the fruit of the Spirit is love, joy, peace, longsuffering, gentleness, goodness, faith,

Meekness, temperance: against such there is no law.

GALATIANS 5:22,23

I am crucified with Christ: nevertheless I live; yet not I, but Christ liveth in me: and the life which I now live in the flesh I live by the faith of the Son of God, who loved me, and gave himself for me.

GALATIANS 2:20

Forgiveness

Who gave himself for our sins, that he might deliver us from this present evil world, according to the will of God and our Father:

GALATIANS 1:4

In whom we have redemption through his blood, the forgiveness of sins, according to the riches of his grace;

EPHESIANS 1:7

Forbearing one another, and forgiving one another, if any man have a quarrel against any: even as Christ forgave you, so also do ye:

COLOSSIANS 3:13

In whom we have redemption through his blood, even the forgiveness of sins:

COLOSSIANS 1:14

For this is my blood of the new testament, which is shed for many for the remission of sins.

MATTHEW 26:28

If we confess our sins, he is faithful and just to forgive us our sins, and to cleanse us from all unrighteousness.

I JOHN 1:9

Blessed is he whose transgression is forgiven, whose sin is covered.

PSALM 32:1

Be ye therefore merciful, as your Father also is merciful.

Judge not, and ye shall not be judged: condemn not, and ye shall not be condemned: forgive, and ye shall be forgiven:

LUKE 6:36,37

But I say unto you, Love your enemies, bless them that curse you, do good to them that hate you, and pray for them which despitefully use you, and persecute you;

That ye may be the children of your Father which is in heaven: for he maketh his sun to rise on the evil and on the good, and sendeth rain on the just and on the unjust.

MATTHEW 5:44,45

For if ye forgive men their trespasses, your heavenly Father will also forgive you:

MATTHEW 6:14

Giving

Give, and it shall be given unto you; good measure, pressed down, and shaken together, and running over, shall men give into your bosom. For with the same measure that ye mete withal it shall be measured to you again.

LUKE 6:38

For God so loved the world, that he gave his only begotten Son, that whosoever believeth in him should not perish,but have everlasting life.

JOHN 3:16

. . . Inasmuch as ye have done it unto one of the least of these my brethren, ye have done it unto me.

MATTHEW 25:40

Blessed is he that considereth the poor: the Lord will deliver him in time of trouble.

PSALM 41:1

There is that scattereth, and yet increaseth; and there is that withholdeth more than is meet, but it tendeth to poverty.

The liberal soul shall be made fat: and he that watereth shall be watered also himself.

PROVERBS 11:24,25

He that hath pity upon the poor lendeth unto the Lord; and that which he hath given will he pay him again.

PROVERBS 19:17

Heal the sick, cleanse the lepers, raise the dead, cast out devils: freely ye have received, freely give.

MATTHEW 10:8

But this I say, He which soweth sparingly shall reap also sparingly; and he which soweth bountifully shall reap also bountifully.

Every man according as he purposeth in his heart, so let him give, not grudgingly, or of necessity: for God loveth a cheerful giver.

And God is able to make all grace abound toward you; that ye, always having all sufficiency in all things, may abound to every good work:

II CORINTHIANS 9:6,7,8

God

For this God is our God for ever and ever: he will be our guide even unto death.

PSALM 48:14

My flesh and my heart faileth: but God is the strength of my heart, and my portion for ever.

PSALM 73:26

Fear thou not; for I am with thee: be not dismayed; for I am thy God: I will strengthen thee; yea, I will help thee; yea, I will uphold thee with the right hand of my righteousness.

ISAIAH 41:10

And ye shall be my people, and I will be your God.

JEREMIAH 30:22

. . . I am thy shield, and thy exceeding great reward.

GENESIS 15:1

But now they desire a better country, that is, an heavenly: wherefore God is not ashamed to be called their God: for he hath prepared for them a city.

HEBREWS 11:16

. . . I will never leave thee, nor forsake thee.

HEBREWS 13:5

. . . Know therefore that God exacteth of thee less than thine iniquity deserveth.

JOB 11:6

What shall we then say to these things? If God be for us, who can be against us?

ROMANS 8:31

God is not a man, that he should lie; neither the son of man, that he should repent: hath he said, and shall he not do it? or hath he spoken, and shall he not make it good?

NUMBERS 23:19

God's Goodness

O give thanks unto the Lord; for he is good; for his mercy endureth for ever.

I CHRONICLES 16:34

Good and upright is the Lord: therefore will he teach sinners in the way.

PSALM 25:8

O taste and see that the Lord is good: blessed is the man that trusteth in him.

PSALM 34:8

For thou, Lord, art good, and ready to forgive; and plenteous in mercy unto all them that call upon thee.

PSALM 86:5

The Lord is good, a strong hold in the day of trouble; and he knoweth them that trust in him.

NAHUM 1:7

That ye may be the children of your Father which is in heaven: for he maketh his sun to rise on the evil and on the good, and sendeth rain on the just and on the unjust.

MATTHEW 5:45

And Jesus said unto him, Why callest thou me good? there is none good but one, that is, God.

MARK 10:18

Enter into his gates with thanksgiving, and into his courts with praise: be thankful unto him, and bless his name.

For the Lord is good; his mercy is everlasting; and his truth endureth to all generations.

PSALM 100:4,5

God's Love

But God commendeth his love toward us, in that, while we were yet sinners, Christ died for us.

ROMANS 5:8

And he will love thee, and bless thee, . . .

DEUTERONOMY 7:13

. . . the Lord loveth the righteous:

PSALM 146:8

Yet the Lord will command his lovingkindness in the daytime, . . .

PSALM 42:8

The Lord hath appeared of old unto me, saying, Yea, I have loved thee with an everlasting love: therefore with lovingkindness have I drawn thee.

JEREMIAH 31:3

Herein is love, not that we loved God, but that he loved us, and sent his Son to be the propitiation for our sins.

And we have known and believed the love that God hath to us. God is love; and he that dwelleth in love dwelleth in God, and God in him.

We love him, because he first loved us.

I JOHN 4:10,16,19

For God so loved the world, that he gave his only begotten Son, that whosoever believeth in him should not perish, but have everlasting life.

JOHN 3:16

For the Father himself loveth you, because ye have loved me, and have believed that I came out from God.

JOHN 16:27

But God, who is rich in mercy, for his great love wherewith he loved us,

Even when we were dead in sins, hath quickened us together with Christ, (by grace ye are saved;)

And hath raised us up together, and made us sit together in heavenly places in Christ Jesus:

That in the ages to come he might shew the exceeding riches of his grace in his kindness toward us through Christ Jesus.

EPHESIANS 2:4,5,6,7

Greed

And he said unto them, Take heed, and beware of covetousness: for a man's life consisteth not in the abundance of the things which he possesseth.

LUKE 12:15

Blessed are the pure in heart: for they shall see God.

MATTHEW 5:8

For we brought nothing into this world, and it is certain we can carry nothing out.

And having food and raiment let us be therewith content.

I TIMOTHY 6:7,8

But fornication, and all uncleanness, or covetousness, let it not be once named among you, as becometh saints:

EPHESIANS 5:3

The Lord rewarded me according to my righteousness: according to the cleanness of my hands hath he recompensed me.

II SAMUEL 22:21

. . . but he that hateth covetousness shall prolong his days.

PROVERBS 28:16

Hatred

Ye have heard that it hath been said, Thou shalt love thy neighbour, and hate thine enemy.

But I say unto you, Love your enemies, bless them that curse you, do good to them that hate you, and pray for them which despitefully use you, and persecute you.

MATTHEW 5:43,44

If the world hate you, ye know that it hated me before it hated you.

He that hateth me hateth my Father also.

JOHN 15:18,23

I have given them thy word; and the world hath hated them, because they are not of the world, even as I am not of the world.

JOHN 17:14

But he that sinneth against me wrongeth his own soul: all they that hate me love death.

PROVERBS 8:36

Shew me a token for good; that they which hate me may see it, and be ashamed: because thou, Lord, hast holpen me, and comforted me.

PSALM 86:17

He that saith he is in the light, and hateth his brother, is in the darkness even until now.

I JOHN 2:9

Heaven

Blessed be the God and Father of our Lord Jesus Christ, which according to his abundant mercy hath begotten us again unto a lively hope by the resurrection of Jesus Christ from the dead.

To an inheritance incorruptible, and undefiled, and that fadeth not away, reserved in heaven for you,

I PETER 1:3,4

Nevertheless we, according to his promise, look for new heavens and a new earth, wherein dwelleth righteousness.

II PETER 3:13

And there shall be no night there; and they need no candle, neither light of the sun; for the Lord God giveth them light: and they shall reign for ever and ever.

REVELATION 22:5

In my Father's house are many mansions: if it were not so, I would have told you. I go to prepare a place for you.

JOHN 14:2

But now they desire a better country, that is, an heavenly: wherefore God is not ashamed to be called their God: for he hath prepared for them a city.

HEBREWS 11:16

Then we which are alive and remain shall be caught up together with them in the clouds, to meet the Lord in the air: and so shall we ever be with the Lord.

Wherefore comfort one another with these words.

I THESSALONIANS 4:17,18

Ye are blessed of the Lord which made heaven and earth..

The heaven, even the heavens, are the Lord's: but the earth hath he given to the children of men.

PSALM 115:15,16

Hell

In flaming fire taking vengeance on them that know not God, and that obey not the gospel of our Lord Jesus Christ:

Who shall be punished with everlasting destruction from the presence of the Lord, and from the glory of his power;

II THESSALONIANS 1:8,9

The wicked shall be turned into hell, and all the nations that forget God.

PSALM 9:17

The way of life is above to the wise, that he may depart from hell beneath.

PROVERBS 15:24

Hell and destruction are never full; so the eyes of man are never satisfied.

PROVERBS 27:20

Therefore hell hath enlarged herself, and opened her mouth without measure: and their glory, and their multitude, and their pomp, and he that rejoiceth, shall descend into it.

ISAIAH 5:14

And in hell he lift up his eyes, being in torments, and seeth Abraham afar off, and Lazarus in his bosom.

LUKE 16:23

The Holy Spirit

And I will pray the Father, and he shall give you another Comforter, that he may abide with you for ever;

Even the Spirit of truth; whom the world cannot receive, because it seeth him not, neither knoweth him: but ye know him; for he dwelleth with you, and shall be in you.

I will not leave you comfortless: I will come to you.

JOHN 14:16,17,18

If ye then, being evil, know how to give good gifts unto your children: how much more shall your heavenly Father give the Holy Spirit to them that ask him?

LUKE 11:13

For the Holy Ghost shall teach you in the same hour what ye ought to say.

LUKE 12:12

In whom ye also trusted, after that ye heard the word of truth, the gospel of your salvation: in whom also after that ye believed, ye were sealed with that holy Spirit of promise,

EPHESIANS 1:13

And grieve not the holy Spirit of God, whereby ye are sealed unto the day of redemption.

EPHESIANS 4:30

And be not drunk with wine, wherein is excess; but be filled with the Spirit;

EPHESIANS 5:18

Now we have received, not the spirit of the world, but the spirit which is of God; that we might know the things that are freely given to us of God.

I CORINTHIANS 2:12

What? know ye not that your body is the temple of the Holy Ghost which is in you, which ye have of God, and ye are not your own?

I CORINTHIANS 6:19

Howbeit when he, the Spirit of truth, is come, he will guide you into all truth: for he shall not speak of himself; but whatsoever he shall hear, that shall he speak: and he will shew you things to come.

JOHN 16:13

And I will put my spirit within you, and cause you to walk in my statutes, and ye shall keep my judgments, and do them.

EZEKIEL 36:27

Hope

Therefore did my heart rejoice, and my tongue was glad; moreover also my flesh shall rest in hope:

ACTS 2:26

For we are saved by hope: but hope that is seen is not hope: for what a man seeth, why doth he yet hope for?

ROMANS 8:24

Blessed be the God and Father of our Lord Jesus Christ, which according to his abundant mercy hath begotten us again unto a lively hope by the resurrection of Jesus Christ from the dead,

I PETER 1:3

Beloved, now are we the sons of God, and it doth not yet appear what we shall be: but we know that, when he shall appear, we shall be like him; for we shall see him as he is.

And every man that hath this hope in him purifieth himself, even as he is pure.

I JOHN 3:2,3

For thou art my hope, O Lord God: thou art my trust from my youth.

PSALM 71:5

Remember the word unto thy servant, upon which thou hast caused me to hope.

PSALM 119:49

. . . which is Christ in you, the hope of glory:

COLOSSIANS 1:27

Be of good courage, and he shall strengthen your heart, all ye that hope in the Lord.

PSALM 31:24

Why art thou cast down, O my soul? and why art thou disquieted within me? hope thou in God: for I shall yet praise him, who is the health of my countenance, and my God.

PSALM 42:11

The wicked is driven away in his wickedness: but the righteous hath hope in his death.

PROVERBS 14:32

Wherefore gird up the loins of your mind, be sober, and hope to the end for the grace that is to be brought unto you at the revelation of Jesus Christ;

Who by him do believe in God, that raised him up from the dead, and gave him glory; that your faith and hope might be in God.

I PETER 1:13,21

Hospitality

Distributing to the necessity of saints; given to hospitality.

ROMANS 12:13

Be not forgetful to entertain strangers: for thereby some have entertained angels unawares.

HEBREWS 13:2

Use hospitality one to another without grudging.

As every man hath received the gift, even so minister the same one to another, as good stewards of the manifold grace of God.

I PETER 4:9,10

Beloved, thou doest faithfully whatsoever thou doest to the brethren, and to strangers;

We therefore ought to receive such, that we might be fellow-helpers to the truth.

III JOHN 1:5,8

He that receiveth a prophet in the name of a prophet shall receive a prophet's reward; and he that receiveth a righteous man in the name of a righteous man shall receive a righteous man's reward.

MATTHEW 10:41

For I was an hungered, and ye gave me meat: I was thirsty, and ye gave me drink: I was a stranger, and ye took me in:

And the King shall answer and say unto them, Verily I say unto you, Inasmuch as ye have done it unto one of the least of these my brethren, ye have done it unto me.

MATTHEW 25:35,40

For I mean not that other men be eased, and ye burdened:

But by an equality, that now at this time your abundance may be a supply for their want, that their abundance also may be a supply for your want: that there may be equality:

II CORINTHIANS 8:13,14

But whoso hath this world's good, and seeth his brother have need, and shutteth up his bowels of compassion from him, how dwelleth the love of God in him?

I JOHN 3:17

For whosoever shall give you a cup of water to drink in my name, because ye belong to Christ, verily I say unto you, he shall not lose his reward.

MARK 9:41

I have shewed you all things, how that so labouring ye ought to support the weak, and to remember the words of the Lord Jesus, how he said, It is more blessed to give than to receive.

ACTS 20:35

As we have therefore opportunity, let us do good unto all men, especially unto them who are of the household of faith.

GALATIANS 6:10

The Human Heart

The heart is deceitful above all things, and desperately wicked: who can know it?

JEREMIAH 17:9

Even so ye also outwardly appear righteous unto men, but within ye are full of hypocrisy and iniquity.

MATTHEW 23:28

And he said, That which cometh out of the man, that defileth the man.

For from within, out of the heart of men, proceed evil thoughts, adulteries, fornications, murders,

All these evil things come from within, and defile the man.

MARK 7:20,21,23

Wherefore God also gave them up to uncleanness through the lusts of their own hearts, to dishonour their own bodies between themselves:

ROMANS 1:24

For to be carnally minded is death; but to be spiritually minded is life and peace.

ROMANS 8:6

They profess that they know God; but in works they deny him, being abominable, and disobedient, and unto every good work reprobate.

TITUS 1:16

And let the peace of God rule in your hearts, to the which also ye are called in one body; and be ye thankful.

COLOSSIANS 3:15

The king's heart is in the hand of the Lord, as the rivers of water: he turneth it whithersoever he will.

Every way of a man is right in his own eyes: but the Lord pondereth the hearts.

To do justice and judgment is more acceptable to the Lord than sacrifice.

An high look, and a proud heart, and the plowing of the wicked, is sin.

PROVERBS 21:1,2,3,4

Human Nature

Because that, when they knew God, they glorified him not as God, neither were thankful; but became vain in their imaginations, and their foolish heart was darkened.

Professing themselves to be wise, they became fools,

And changed the glory of the uncorruptible God into an image made like to corruptible man, and to birds, and fourfooted beasts, and creeping things.

Wherefore God also gave them up to uncleanness through the lusts of their own hearts, to dishonour their own bodies between themselves:

Who changed the truth of God into a lie, and worshipped and served the creature more than the Creator, who is blessed for ever. Amen.

And even as they did not like to retain God in their knowledge, God gave them over to a reprobate mind, to do those things which are not convenient;

ROMANS 1:21-25,28

This know also, that in the last days perilous times shall come.

For men shall be lovers of their own selves, covetous, boasters, proud, blasphemers, disobedient to parents, unthankful, unholy,

Without natural affection, trucebreakers, false accusers, incontinent, fierce, despisers of those that are good,

Traitors, heady, highminded, lovers of pleasures more than lovers of God;

Having a form of godliness, but denying the power thereof: from such turn away.

Ever learning, and never able to come to the knowledge of the truth.

II TIMOTHY 3:1-5,7

Immorality

Which forsaketh the guide of her youth, and forgetteth the covenant of her God.

For her house inclineth unto death, and her paths unto the dead.

PROVERBS 2:17,18

And thou mourn at the last, when thy flesh and thy body are consumed,

And say, How have I hated instruction, and my heart despised reproof;

And have not obeyed the voice of my teachers, nor inclined mine ear to them that instructed me!

For the ways of man are before the eyes of the Lord, and he pondereth all his goings.

PROVERBS 5:11-13,21

For by means of a whorish woman a man is brought to a piece of bread: and the adulteress will hunt for the precious life.

Can a man take fire in his bosom, and his clothes not be burned?

But whoso committeth adultery with a woman lacketh understanding: he that doeth it destroyeth his own soul.

PROVERBS 6:26,27,32

He goeth after her straightway, as an ox goeth to the slaughter, or as a fool to the correction of the stocks;

Till a dart strike through his liver; as a bird hasteth to the snare, and knoweth not that it is for his life.

Her house is the way to hell, going down to the chambers of death.

PROVERBS 7:22,23,27

But he knoweth not that the dead are there; and that her guests are in the depths of hell.

PROVERBS 9:18

Joy

The Lord is my strength and my shield; my heart trusted in him, and I am helped: therefore my heart greatly rejoiceth; and with my song will I praise him.

PSALM 28:7

But let the righteous be glad; let them rejoice before God: yea, let them exceedingly rejoice.

PSALM 68:3

Make a joyful noise unto the Lord, all ye lands.

Serve the Lord with gladness: come before his presence with singing.

PSALM 100:1,2

These things have I spoken unto you, that my joy might remain in you, and that your joy might be full.

JOHN 15:11

In thy name shall they rejoice all the day: and in thy righteousness shall they be exalted.

PSALM 89:16

Rejoice in the Lord alway: and again I say, Rejoice.

PHILIPPIANS 4:4

Yet I will rejoice in the Lord, I will joy in the God of my salvation.

HABAKKUK 3:18

For our heart shall rejoice in him, because we have trusted in his holy name.

PSALM 33:21

And ye now therefore have sorrow: but I will see you again, and your heart shall rejoice, and your joy no man taketh from you.

JOHN 16:22

My soul shall be satisfied as with marrow and fatness; and my mouth shall praise thee with joyful lips:

PSALM 63:5

Whom having not seen, ye love; in whom, though now ye see him not, yet believing, ye rejoice with joy unspeakable and full of glory:

I PETER 1:8

For ye shall go out with joy, and be led forth with peace: the mountains and the hills shall break forth before you into singing, and all the trees of the field shall clap their hands.

ISAIAH 55:12

They that sow in tears shall reap in joy.

He that goeth forth and weepeth, bearing precious seed, shall doubtless come again with rejoicing, bringing his sheaves with him.

PSALM 126:5,6

Judgment

And I saw the dead, small and great, stand before God; and the books were opened: and another book was opened, which is the book of life: and the dead were judged out of those things which were written in the books, according to their works.

REVELATION 20:12

And as it is appointed unto men once to die, but after this the judgment:

HEBREWS 9:27

Judge not, that ye be not judged.

For with what judgment ye judge, ye shall be judged: and with what measure ye mete, it shall be measured to you again.

MATTHEW 7:1,2

For the Father judgeth no man, but hath committed all judgment unto the Son:

JOHN 5:22

For God shall bring every work into judgment, with every secret thing, whether it be good, or whether it be evil.

ECCLESIASTES 12:14

Evil men understand not judgment: but they that seek the Lord understand all things.

PROVERBS 28:5

Life

For length of days, and long life, and peace, shall they add to thee.

PROVERBS 3:2

Surely goodness and mercy shall follow me all the days of my life: and I will dwell in the house of the Lord for ever.

PSALM 23:6

And Satan answered the Lord, and said, Skin for skin, yea, all that a man hath will he give for his life.

JOB 2:4

In him was life; and the life was the light of men.

JOHN 1:4

The thief cometh not, but for to steal, and to kill, and to destroy: I am come that they might have life, and that they might have it more abundantly.

JOHN 10:10

For whosoever will save his life shall lose it; but whosoever shall lose his life for my sake and the gospel's, the same shall save it.

MARK 8:35

For to be carnally minded is death; but to be spiritually minded is life and peace.

ROMANS 8:6

But he, being full of compassion, forgave their iniquity, and destroyed them not: yea, many a time turned he his anger away, and did not stir up all his wrath.

For he remembered that they were but flesh; a wind that passeth away, and cometh not again.

PSALM 78:38,39

Whereas ye know not what shall be on the morrow. For what is your life? It is even a vapour, that appeareth for a little time, and then vanisheth away.

JAMES 4:14

As for man, his days are as grass: as a flower of the field, so he flourisheth.

For the wind passeth over it, and it is gone; and the place thereof shall know it no more.

PSALM 103:15,16

Loneliness

I will not leave you comfortless: I will come to you.

JOHN 14:18

. . . for he hath said, I will never leave thee, nor forsake thee.

HEBREWS 13:5

Draw nigh to God, and he will draw nigh to you. . . .

JAMES 4:8

. . . and truly our fellowship is with the Father, and with his Son Jesus Christ.

I JOHN 1:3

A man that hath friends must shew himself friendly: and there is a friend that sticketh closer than a brother.

PROVERBS 18:24

When my father and my mother forsake me, then the Lord will take me up.

PSALM 27:10

. . . These things will I do unto them, and not forsake them.

ISAIAH 42:16

Behold, I stand at the door, and knock: if any man hear my voice, and open the door, I will come in to him, and will sup with him, and he with me.

REVELATION 3:20

Then shalt thou call, and the Lord shall answer; thou shalt cry, and he shall say, Here I am. . . .

ISAIAH 58:9

And, behold, I am with thee, and will keep thee in all places whither thou goest, and will bring thee again into this land; for I will not leave thee, until I have done that which I have spoken to thee of.

GENESIS 28:15

Man

And needed not that any should testify of man:
for he knew what was in man.

JOHN 2:25

So God created man in his own image, in the
image of God created he him; male and female
created he them.

GENESIS 1:27

And the Lord God said, It is not good that the
man should be alone; I will make him an help
meet for him.

GENESIS 2:18

Blessed is the man that walketh not in the counsel
of the ungodly, nor standeth in the way of sinners,
nor sitteth in the seat of the scornful.

PSALM 1:1

The steps of a good man are ordered by the
Lord: and he delighteth in his way.

PSALM 37:23

No man can serve two masters: for either he
will hate the one, and love the other; or else
he will hold to the one, and despise the other.
Ye cannot serve God and mammon.

MATTHEW 6:24

Let us hear the conclusion of the whole matter:
Fear God, and keep his commandments: for this
is the whole duty of man.

ECCLESIASTES 12:13

Marriage

But from the beginning of the creation God made them male and female.

For this cause shall a man leave his father and mother, and cleave to his wife;

And they twain shall be one flesh: so then they are no more twain, but one flesh.

What therefore God hath joined together, let not man put asunder.

MARK 10:6-9

Submitting yourselves one to another in the fear of God.

Wives, submit yourselves unto your own husbands, as unto the Lord.

For the husband is the head of the wife, even as Christ is the head of the church: and he is the saviour of the body.

Therefore as the church is subject unto Christ, so let the wives be to their own husbands in every thing.

Husbands, love your wives, even as Christ also loved the church, and gave himself for it;

That he might sanctify and cleanse it with the washing of water by the word,

EPHESIANS 5:21-26

Whoso findeth a wife findeth a good thing, and obtaineth favour of the Lord.

PROVERBS 18:22

Drink waters out of thine own cistern, and running waters out of thine own well.

PROVERBS 5:15

But if any provide not for his own, and specially for those of his own house, he hath denied the faith, and is worse than an infidel.

I TIMOTHY 5:8

Likewise, ye husbands, dwell with them according to knowledge, giving honour unto the wife, as unto the weaker vessel, and as being heirs together of the grace of life; that your prayers be not hindered.

I PETER 3:7

That they may teach the young women to be sober, to love their husbands, to love their children,

To be discreet, chaste, keepers at home, good, obedient to their own husbands, that the word of God be not blasphemed.

TITUS 2:4,5

Let thy fountain be blessed: and rejoice with the wife of thy youth.

Let her be as the loving hind and pleasant roe; let her breasts satisfy thee at all times; and be thou ravished always with her love.

PROVERBS 5:18,19

Mercy

But God, who is rich in mercy, for his great love wherewith he loved us,

EPHESIANS 2:4

. . . I will have mercy on whom I will have mercy, and I will have compassion on whom I will have compassion.

ROMANS 9:15

And his mercy is on them that fear him from generation to generation.

LUKE 1:50

Be ye therefore merciful, as your Father also is merciful.

LUKE 6:36

Blessed are the merciful: for they shall obtain mercy.

MATTHEW 5:7

He that despiseth his neighbour sinneth: but he that hath mercy on the poor, happy is he.

PROVERBS 14:21

Hear, O Lord, when I cry with my voice: have mercy also upon me, and answer me.

PSALM 27:7

Be merciful unto me, O Lord: for I cry unto thee daily.

For thou, Lord, art good, and ready to forgive; and plenteous in mercy unto all them that call upon thee.

PSALM 86:3,5

. . . Know therefore that God exacteth of thee less than thine iniquity deserveth.

JOB 11:6

. . . for in my wrath I smote thee, but in my favour have I had mercy on thee.

ISAIAH 60:10

Like as a father pitieth his children, so the Lord pitieth them that fear him.

PSALM 103:13

And he said, I will make all my goodness pass before thee, and I will proclaim the name of the Lord before thee; and will be gracious to whom I will be gracious, and will shew mercy on whom I will shew mercy.

EXODUS 33:19

Obedience

For as by one man's disobedience many were
made sinners, so by the obedience of one shall
many be made righteous.

ROMANS 5:19

Let every soul be subject unto the higher powers.
For there is no power but of God: the powers
that be are ordained of God.

Render therefore to all their dues: tribute to
whom tribute is due; custom to whom custom;
fear to whom fear; honour to whom honour.

ROMANS 13:1,7

Know ye not, that to whom ye yield yourselves
servants to obey, his servants ye are to whom
ye obey; whether of sin unto death, or of
obedience unto righteousness?

ROMANS 6:16

But now is made manifest, and by the scriptures
of the prophets, according to the commandment
of the everlasting God, made known to all nations
for the obedience of faith:

ROMANS 16:26

Then Peter and the other apostles answered and
said, We ought to obey God rather than men.

ACTS 5:29

. . . what shall the end be of them that obey not the gospel of God?

I PETER 4:17

Verily, verily, I say unto you, If a man keep my saying, he shall never see death.

JOHN 8:51

And the world passeth away, and the lust thereof: but he that doeth the will of God abideth for ever.

I JOHN 2:17

If ye know these things, happy are ye if ye do them.

JOHN 13:17

If ye keep my commandments, ye shall abide in my love; even as I have kept my Father's commandments, and abide in his love.

JOHN 15:10

If they obey and serve him, they shall spend their days in prosperity, and their years in pleasures.

JOB 36:11

Those things, which ye have both learned, and received, and heard, and seen in me, do: and the God of peace shall be with you.

PHILIPPIANS 4:9

Keep therefore the words of this covenant, and do them, that ye may prosper in all that ye do.

DEUTERONOMY 29:9

Praise

Therefore I will give thanks unto thee, O Lord, among the heathen, and I will sing praises unto thy name.

II SAMUEL 22:50

I will praise thee, O Lord, with my whole heart; I will shew forth all thy marvellous works.

PSALM 9:1

Praise ye the Lord: for it is good to sing praises unto our God; for it is pleasant; and praise is comely.

PSALM 147:1

And in that day shall ye say, Praise the Lord, call upon his name, declare his doings among the people, make mention that his name is exalted.

ISAIAH 12:4

And Mary said, My soul doth magnify the Lord, And my spirit hath rejoiced in God my Saviour.

LUKE 1:46,47

Praise ye the Lord. O give thanks unto the Lord; for he is good: for his mercy endureth for ever.

PSALM 106:1

Make a joyful noise unto the Lord, all ye lands.

Serve the Lord with gladness: come before his presence with singing.

Know ye that the Lord he is God: it is he that hath made us, and not we ourselves; we are his people, and the sheep of his pasture.

Enter into his gates with thanksgiving, and into his courts with praise: be thankful unto him, and bless his name.

For the Lord is good; his mercy is everlasting; and his truth endureth to all generations.

PSALM 100

Praise ye the Lord. Praise God in his sanctuary: praise him in the firmament of his power.

Praise him for his mighty acts: praise him according to his excellent greatness.

Praise him with the sound of the trumpet: praise him with the psaltery and harp.

Praise him with the timbrel and dance: praise him with stringed instruments and organs.

Praise him upon the loud cymbals: praise him upon the high sounding cymbals.

Let every thing that hath breath praise the Lord. Praise ye the Lord.

PSALM 150

Prayer

And call upon me in the day of trouble: I will deliver thee, and thou shalt glorify me.

PSALM 50:15

The Lord is far from the wicked: but he heareth the prayer of the righteous.

PROVERBS 15:29

And it shall come to pass, that before they call, I will answer; and while they are yet speaking, I will hear.

ISAIAH 65:24

Call unto me, and I will answer thee, and shew thee great and mighty things, which thou knowest not.

JEREMIAH 33:3

Thou shalt make thy prayer unto him, and he shall hear thee . . .

JOB 22:27

And in all things, whatsoever ye shall ask in prayer, believing, ye shall receive.

MATTHEW 21:22

Therefore I say unto you, What things soever ye desire, when ye pray, believe that ye receive them, and ye shall have them.

MARK 11:24

Evening, and morning, and at noon, will I pray, and cry aloud: and he shall hear my voice.

PSALM 55:17

If ye abide in me, and my words abide in you, ye shall ask what ye will, and it shall be done unto you.

JOHN 15:7

But thou, when thou prayest, enter into thy closet, and when thou hast shut thy door, pray to thy Father which is in secret; and thy Father which seeth in secret shall reward thee openly.

Be not ye therefore like unto them: for your Father knoweth what things ye have need of, before ye ask him.

MATTHEW 6:6,8

Ask, and it shall be given you; seek, and ye shall find; knock, and it shall be opened unto you:

For every one that asketh receiveth; and he that seeketh findeth; and to him that knocketh it shall be opened.

If ye then, being evil, know how to give good gifts unto your children, how much more shall your Father which is in heaven give good things to them that ask him?

MATTHEW 7:7,8,11

Let us therefore come boldly unto the throne of grace, that we may obtain mercy, and find grace to help in time of need.

HEBREWS 4:16

And this is the confidence that we have in him, that, if we ask any thing according to his will, he heareth us:

And if we know that he hear us, whatsoever we ask, we know that we have the petitions that we desired of him.

I JOHN 5:14,15

Purity

Blessed are the pure in heart: for they shall see God.

MATTHEW 5:8

Now the end of the commandment is charity out of a pure heart, and of a good conscience, and of faith unfeigned:

I TIMOTHY 1:5

Let no man despise thy youth; but be thou an example of the believers, in word, in conversation, in charity, in spirit, in faith, in purity.

I TIMOTHY 4:12

Flee also youthful lusts: but follow righteousness, faith, charity, peace, with them that call on the Lord out of a pure heart.

II TIMOTHY 2:22

Unto the pure all things are pure: but unto them that are defiled and unbelieving is nothing pure; but even their mind and conscience is defiled.

TITUS 1:15

Pure religion and undefiled before God and the Father is this, To visit the fatherless and widows in their affliction, and to keep himself unspotted from the world.

JAMES 1:27

Repentance

And the publican, standing afar off, would not lift up so much as his eyes unto heaven, but smote upon his breast, saying, God be merciful to me a sinner.

LUKE 18:13

And that repentance and remission of sins should be preached in his name among all nations, beginning at Jerusalem.

LUKE 24:47

And saying, Repent ye: for the kingdom of heaven is at hand.

MATTHEW 3:2

When Jesus heard it, he saith unto them, They that are whole have no need of the physician, but they that are sick: I came not to call the righteous, but sinners to repentance.

MARK 2:17

And they went out, and preached that men should repent.

MARK 6:12

. . . not knowing that the goodness of God leadeth thee to repentance?

ROMANS 2:4

For godly sorrow worketh repentance to salvation not to be repented of: but the sorrow of the world worketh death.

II CORINTHIANS 7:10

. . . but is longsuffering to us-ward, not willing that any should perish, but that all should come to repentance.

II PETER 3:9

The Lord is nigh unto them that are of a broken heart; and saveth such as be of a contrite spirit.

PSALM 34:18

. . . for I am not come to call the righteous, but sinners to repentance.

MATTHEW 9:13

The Resurrection

Beginning from the baptism of John, unto that same day that he was taken up from us, must one be ordained to be a witness with us of his resurrection.

ACTS 1:22

And with great power gave the apostles witness of the resurrection of the Lord Jesus: and great grace was upon them all.

ACTS 4:33

Martha said unto him, I know that he shall rise again in the resurrection at the last day.

Jesus said unto her, I am the resurrection, and the life: he that believeth in me, though he were dead, yet shall he live:

JOHN 11:24,25

For I delivered unto you first of all that which I also received, how that Christ died for our sins according to the scriptures;

And that he was buried, and that he rose again the third day according to the scriptures:

But now is Christ risen from the dead, and become the first-fruits of them that slept.

I CORINTHIANS 15:3,4,20

That I may know him, and the power of his resurrection, and the fellowship of his sufferings, being made conformable unto his death;

PHILIPPIANS 3:10

For if we have been planted together in the likeness of his death, we shall be also in the likeness of his resurrection:

ROMANS 6:5

Blessed be the God and Father of our Lord Jesus Christ, which according to his abundant mercy hath begotten us again unto a lively hope by the resurrection of Jesus Christ from the dead,

To an inheritance incorruptible, and undefiled, and that fadeth not away, reserved in heaven for you,

Who are kept by the power of God through faith unto salvation ready to be revealed in the last time.

I PETER 1:3,4,5

But the rest of the dead lived not again until the thousand years were finished. This is the first resurrection.

Blessed and holy is he that hath part in the first resurrection: on such the second death hath no power, but they shall be priests of God and of Christ, and shall reign with him a thousand years.

REVELATION 20:5,6

Revenge

It is God that avengeth me, and subdueth the people under me.

PSALM 18:47

Cease from anger, and forsake wrath: fret not thyself in any wise to do evil.

PSALM 37:8

A stone is heavy, and the sand weighty; but a fool's wrath is heavier than them both.

PROVERBS 27:3

Ye have heard that it hath been said, An eye for an eye, and a tooth for a tooth:

But I say unto you, That ye resist not evil: but whosoever shall smite thee on thy right cheek, turn to him the other also.

MATTHEW 5:38,39

And shall not God avenge his own elect, which cry day and night unto him, though he bear long with them?

LUKE 18:7

Dearly beloved, avenge not yourselves, but rather give place unto wrath: for it is written, Vengeance is mine; I will repay, saith the Lord.

ROMANS 12:19

Be ye angry, and sin not; let not the sun go down upon your wrath:

EPHESIANS 4:26

Riches

A little that a righteous man hath is better than the riches of many wicked.

PSALM 37:16

Trust not in oppression, and become not vain in robbery: if riches increase, set not your heart upon them.

PSALM 62:10

Riches profit not in the day of wrath: but righteousness delivereth from death.

He that trusteth in his riches shall fall: but the righteous shall flourish as a branch.

PROVERBS 11:4,28

There is that maketh himself rich, yet hath nothing: there is that maketh himself poor, yet hath great riches.

PROVERBS 13:7

A good name is rather to be chosen than great riches, and loving favour rather than silver and gold.

PROVERBS 22:1

Wilt thou set thine eyes upon that which is not? for riches certainly make themselves wings; they fly away as an eagle toward heaven.

PROVERBS 23:5

For riches are not for ever: and doth the crown endure to every generation?

PROVERBS 27:24

Remove far from me vanity and lies: give me neither poverty nor riches; feed me with food convenient for me:

PROVERBS 30:8

Thus saith the Lord, Let not the wise man glory in his wisdom, neither let the mighty man glory in his might, let not the rich man glory in his riches:

But let him that glorieth glory in this, that he understandeth and knoweth me, that I am the Lord which exercise lovingkindness, judgment, and righteousness, in the earth: for in these things I delight, saith the Lord.

JEREMIAH 9:23,24

Lay not up for yourselves treasures upon earth, where moth and rust doth corrupt, and where thieves break through and steal:

But lay up for yourselves treasures in heaven. . .

For where your treasure is, there will your heart be also.

MATTHEW 6:19,20,21

. . . How hardly shall they that have riches enter into the kingdom of God!

It is easier for a camel to go through the eye of a needle, than for a rich man to enter into the kingdom of God.

MARK 10:23,25

Charge them that are rich in this world, that they be not highminded, nor trust in uncertain riches, but in the living God, who giveth us richly all things to enjoy;

That they do good, that they be rich in good works, ready to distribute, willing to communicate;

Laying up in store for themselves a good foundation against the time to come, that they may lay hold on eternal life.

I TIMOTHY 6:17,18,19

Sickness

. . . for I am the Lord that healeth thee.

EXODUS 15:26

And ye shall serve the Lord your God, and he shall bless thy bread, and thy water; and I will take sickness away from the midst of thee.

EXODUS 23:25

The Lord will strengthen him upon the bed of languishing: thou wilt make all his bed in his sickness.

PSALM 41:3

But he was wounded for our transgressions, he was bruised for our iniquities: the chastisement of our peace was upon him; and with his stripes we are healed.

ISAIAH 53:5

Heal me, O Lord, and I shall be healed; save me, and I shall be saved: for thou art my praise.

JEREMIAH 17:14

For I will restore health unto thee, and I will heal thee of thy wounds, saith the Lord; . . .

JEREMIAH 30:17

For our light affliction, which is but for a moment, worketh for us a far more exceeding and eternal weight of glory;

II CORINTHIANS 4:17

And the prayer of faith shall save the sick, and the Lord shall raise him up; . . .

JAMES 5:15

Sin

Behold, the Lord's hand is not shortened, that it cannot save; neither his ear heavy, that it cannot hear:

But your iniquities have separated between you and your God, and your sins have hid his face from you, that he will not hear.

ISAIAH 59:1,2

Blessed is he whose transgression is forgiven, whose sin is covered.

PSALM 32:1

For I will declare mine iniquity; I will be sorry for my sin.

PSALM 38:18

For I acknowledge my transgressions: and my sin is ever before me.

Behold, I was shapen in iniquity, and in sin did my mother conceive me.

PSALM 51:3,5

Righteousness exalteth a nation: but sin is a reproach to any people.

PROVERBS 14:34

So when they continued asking him, he lifted up himself, and said unto them, He that is without sin among you, let him first cast a stone at her.

Jesus answered them, Verily, verily, I say unto you, Whosoever committeth sin is the servant of sin.

JOHN 8:7,34

As it is written, There is none righteous, no, not one:

For all have sinned, and come short of the glory of God;

ROMANS 3:10,23

Wherefore, as by one man sin entered into the world, and death by sin; and so death passed upon all men, for that all have sinned:

ROMANS 5:12

Let not sin therefore reign in your mortal body, that ye should obey it in the lusts thereof.

For the wages of sin is death; but the gift of God is eternal life through Jesus Christ our Lord.

ROMANS 6:12,23

For if we sin wilfully after that we have received the knowledge of the truth, there remaineth no more sacrifice for sins,

HEBREWS 10:26

Wherefore seeing we also are compassed about with so great a cloud of witnesses, let us lay aside every weight, and the sin which doth so easily beset us, and let us run with patience the race that is set before us,

HEBREWS 12:1

Then when lust hath conceived, it bringeth forth sin: and sin, when it is finished, bringeth forth death.

JAMES 1:15

Therefore to him that knoweth to do good, and doeth it not, to him it is sin.

JAMES 4:17

If we say that we have no sin, we deceive ourselves, and the truth is not in us.

I JOHN 1:8

My little children, these things write I unto you, that ye sin not. And if any man sin, we have an advocate with the Father, Jesus Christ the righteous:

And he is the propitiation for our sins: and not for ours only, but also for the sins of the whole world.

I JOHN 2:1,2

He that committeth sin is of the devil; for the devil sinneth from the beginning. For this purpose the Son of God was manifested, that he might destroy the works of the devil.

I JOHN 3:8

Strong Drink

Wine is a mocker, strong drink is raging: and whosoever is deceived thereby is not wise.

PROVERBS 20:1

Who hath woe? who hath sorrow? who hath contentions? who hath babbling? who hath wounds without cause? who hath redness of eyes?

They that tarry long at the wine; they that go to seek mixed wine.

At the last it biteth like a serpent, and stingeth like an adder.

Thine eyes shall behold strange women, and thine heart shall utter perverse things.

Yea, thou shalt be as he that lieth down in the midst of the sea, or as he that lieth upon the top of a mast.

They have stricken me, shalt thou say, and I was not sick; they have beaten me, and I felt it not: when shall I awake? I will seek it yet again.

PROVERBS 23:29,30,32-35

It is not for kings, O Lemuel, it is not for kings to drink wine; nor for princes strong drink:

Lest they drink, and forget the law, and pervert the judgment of any of the afflicted.

PROVERBS 31:4,5

Thankfulness

Give thanks unto the Lord, call upon his name, make known his deeds among the people.

I CHRONICLES 16:8

That I may publish with the voice of thanksgiving, and tell of all thy wondrous works.

PSALM 26:7

Sing unto the Lord, O ye saints of his, and give thanks at the remembrance of his holiness.

PSALM 30:4

Let us come before his presence with thanksgiving, . . .

PSALM 95:2

Sing unto the Lord; for he hath done excellent things: this is known in all the earth.

ISAIAH 12:5

And one of them, when he saw that he was healed, turned back, and with a loud voice glorified God,

And fell down on his face at his feet, giving him thanks: and he was a Samaritan.

LUKE 17:15,16

Rejoice evermore.

Pray without ceasing.

In every thing give thanks: for this is the will of God in Christ Jesus concerning you.

I THESSALONIANS 5:16,17,18

Giving thanks always for all things unto God and the Father in the name of our Lord Jesus Christ;

EPHESIANS 5:20

The Tongue

The tongue of the just is as choice silver: the heart of the wicked is little worth.

PROVERBS 10:20

He that is void of wisdom despiseth his neighbour: but a man of understanding holdeth his peace.

PROVERBS 11:12

There is that speaketh like the piercings of a sword: but the tongue of the wise is health.

PROVERBS 12:18

He that keepeth his mouth keepeth his life: but he that openeth wide his lips shall have destruction.

PROVERBS 13:3

A true witness delivereth souls: but a deceitful witness speaketh lies.

PROVERBS 14:25

A soft answer turneth away wrath: but grievous words stir up anger.

A wholesome tongue is a tree of life: but perverseness therein is a breach in the spirit.

A man hath joy by the answer of his mouth: and a word spoken in due season, how good is it!

PROVERBS 15:1,4,23

The heart of the righteous studieth to answer: but the mouth of the wicked poureth out evil things.

PROVERBS 15:28

Pleasant words are as an honeycomb, sweet to the soul, and health to the bones.

A froward man soweth strife: and a whisperer separateth chief friends.

PROVERBS 16:24,28

The words of a talebearer are as wounds, and they go down into the innermost parts of the belly.

He that answereth a matter before he heareth it, it is folly and shame unto him.

Death and life are in the power of the tongue: and they that love it shall eat the fruit thereof.

PROVERBS 18:8,13,21

Whoso keepeth his mouth and his tongue keepeth his soul from troubles.

PROVERBS 21:23

A word fitly spoken is like apples of gold in pictures of silver.

PROVERBS 25:11

He that passeth by, and meddleth with strife belonging not to him, is like one that taketh a dog by the ears.

PROVERBS 26:17

Where no wood is, there the fire goeth out: so where there is no talebearer, the strife ceaseth.

PROVERBS 26:20

Let another man praise thee, and not thine own mouth; a stranger, and not thine own lips.

PROVERBS 27:2

Even so the tongue is a little member, and boasteth great things. Behold, how great a matter a little fire kindleth!

But the tongue can no man tame; it is an unruly evil, full of deadly poison.

JAMES 3:5,8

Truthfulness

Behold, thou desirest truth in the inward parts: and in the hidden part thou shalt make me to know wisdom.

PSALM 51:6

Righteous lips are the delight of kings; and they love him that speaketh right.

PROVERBS 16:13

. . . for all things that I have heard of my Father I have made known unto you.

JOHN 15:15

Howbeit when he, the Spirit of truth, is come, he will guide you into all truth: . . .

JOHN 16:13

Sanctify them through thy truth: thy word is truth.

JOHN 17:17

Wherefore putting away lying, speak every man truth with his neighbour: for we are members one of another.

EPHESIANS 4:25

Lie not one to another, seeing that ye have put off the old man with his deeds;

COLOSSIANS 3:9

Of his own will begat he us with the word of truth, that we should be a kind of firstfruits of his creatures.

JAMES 1:18

Woman

And Adam said, This is now bone of my bones, and flesh of my flesh: she shall be called Woman, because she was taken out of Man.

GENESIS 2:23

A gracious woman retaineth honour: . . .

PROVERBS 11:16

A virtuous woman is a crown to her husband: but she that maketh ashamed is as rottenness in his bones.

PROVERBS 12:4

Who can find a virtuous woman? for her price is far above rubies.

Favour is deceitful, and beauty is vain: but a woman that feareth the Lord, she shall be praised.

PROVERBS 31:10,30

Verily I say unto you, Wheresoever this gospel shall be preached in the whole world, there shall also this, that this woman hath done, be told for a memorial of her.

MATTHEW 26:13

But I would have you know, that the head of every man is Christ; and the head of the woman is the man; and the head of Christ is God.

I CORINTHIANS 11:3

THE
BIBLE IS . . .

A Fire

Wherefore thus saith the Lord God of hosts, Because ye speak this word, behold, I will make my words in thy mouth fire, . . .

JEREMIAH 5:14

Then I said, I will not make mention of him, nor speak any more in his name. But his word was in mine heart as a burning fire shut up in my bones, and I was weary with forbearing, and I could not stay.

JEREMIAH 20:9

Is not my word like as a fire? saith the Lord; . . .

JEREMIAH 23:29

A Mirror

For if any be a hearer of the word, and not a doer, he is like unto a man beholding his natural face in a glass:

For he beholdeth himself, and goeth his way, and straightway forgetteth what manner of man he was.

But whoso looketh into the perfect law of liberty, and continueth therein, he being not a forgetful hearer, but a doer of the work, this man shall be blessed in his deed.

JAMES 1:23,24,25

A Seed

He that goeth forth and weepeth, bearing precious seed, shall doubtless come again with rejoicing, bringing his sheaves with him.

PSALM 126:6

Is the seed yet in the barn? . . .

HAGGAI 2:19

Now the parable is this: The seed is the word of God.

LUKE 8:11

Now he that ministereth seed to the sower both minister bread for your food, and multiply your seed sown, and increase the fruits of your righteousness;

II CORINTHIANS 9:10

Being born again, not of corruptible seed, but of incorruptible, by the word of God, which liveth and abideth for ever.

I PETER 1:23

A Hammer

Is not my word like as a fire? saith the Lord; and like a hammer that breaketh the rock in pieces?

JEREMIAH 23:29

A Lamp

For thou art my lamp, O Lord: and the Lord will lighten my darkness.

II SAMUEL 22:29

Thy word is a lamp unto my feet, and a light unto my path.

PSALM 119:105

For the commandment is a lamp; and the law is light; . . .

PROVERBS 6:23

We have also a more sure word of prophecy; whereunto ye do well that ye take heed, as unto a light that shineth in a dark place, until the day dawn, and the day star arise in your hearts:

II PETER 1:19

Again, a new commandment I write unto you, which thing is true in him and in you: because the darkness is past, and the true light now shineth.

I JOHN 2:8

A Sword

And take the helmet of salvation, and the sword of the Spirit, which is the word of God:

EPHESIANS 6:17

For the word of God is quick, and powerful, and sharper than any two-edged sword, piercing even to the dividing asunder of soul and spirit, and of the joints and marrow, and is a discerner of the thoughts and intents of the heart.

HEBREWS 4:12

Pure

The words of the Lord are pure words: as silver tried in a furnace of earth, purified seven times.

PSALM 12:6

Thy word is very pure: therefore thy servant loveth it.

PSALM 119:140

Every word of God is pure: he is a shield unto them that put their trust in him.

PROVERBS 30:5

Wherefore the law is holy, and the commandment holy, and just, and good.

ROMANS 7:12

Food

Neither have I gone back from the command-ment of his lips; I have esteemed the words of his mouth more than my necessary food.

JOB 23:12

How sweet are thy words unto my taste! yea, sweeter than honey to my mouth!

PSALM 119:103

... It is written, Man shall not live by bread alone, but by every word that proceedeth out of the mouth of God.

MATTHEW 4:4

I have fed you with milk, and not with meat: for hitherto ye were not able to bear it, neither yet now are ye able.

I CORINTHIANS 3:2

As newborn babes, desire the sincere milk of the word, that ye may grow thereby:

If so be ye have tasted that the Lord is gracious.

I PETER 2:2,3

Trustworthy

As for God, his way is perfect; the word of the Lord is tried: he is a buckler to all them that trust in him.

II SAMUEL 22:31

The law of the Lord is perfect, converting the soul: the testimony of the Lord is sure, making wise the simple.

PSALM 19:7

Therefore I esteem all thy precepts concerning all things to be right; and I hate every false way.

PSALM 119:128

Sanctify them through thy truth: thy word is truth.

JOHN 17:17

This is the disciple which testifieth of these things, and wrote these things: and we know that his testimony is true.

JOHN 21:24

And he that sat upon the throne said, Behold, I make all things new. And he said unto me, Write: for these words are true and faithful.

REVELATION 21:5

Divinely Inspired

And the Lord spake by his servants the prophets, saying,

II KINGS 21:10

Thou camest down also upon mount Sinai, and spakest with them from heaven, and gavest them right judgments, and true laws, good statutes and commandments:

NEHEMIAH 9:13

But I certify you, brethren, that the gospel which was preached of me is not after man.

For I neither received it of man, neither was I taught it, but by the revelation of Jesus Christ.

GALATIANS 1:11,12

All scripture is given by inspiration of God, and is profitable for doctrine, for reproof, for correction, for instruction in righteousness:

II TIMOTHY 3:16

For the prophecy came not in old time by the will of man: but holy men of God spake as they were moved by the Holy Ghost.

II PETER 1:21

If we receive the witness of men, the witness of God is greater: for this is the witness of God which he hath testified of his Son.

I JOHN 5:9

BLESSINGS PROMISED TO BELIEVERS . . .

Divine Protection

And, behold, I am with thee, and will keep thee in all places whither thou goest, and will bring thee again into this land; for I will not leave thee, until I have done that which I have spoken to thee of.

GENESIS 28:15

. . . The beloved of the Lord shall dwell in safety by him; and the Lord shall cover him all the day long, and he shall dwell between his shoulders.

DEUTERONOMY 33:12

I will both lay me down in peace, and sleep: for thou, Lord, only makest me dwell in safety.

PSALM 4:8

The Lord is my light and my salvation; whom shall I fear? the Lord is the strength of my life; of whom shall I be afraid?

PSALM 27:1

God is our refuge and strength, a very present help in trouble.

PSALM 46:1

He that dwelleth in the secret place of the most High shall abide under the shadow of the Almighty.

I will say of the Lord, He is my refuge and my fortress: my God; in him will I trust.

PSALM 91:1,2

He shall not be afraid of evil tidings: his heart is fixed, trusting in the Lord.

PSALM 112:7

Our help is in the name of the Lord, who made heaven and earth.

PSALM 124:8

As the mountains are round about Jerusalem, so the Lord is round about his people from henceforth even for ever.

PSALM 125:2

But whoso hearkeneth unto me shall dwell safely, and shall be quiet from fear of evil.

PROVERBS 1:33

Then shalt thou walk in thy way safely, and thy foot shall not stumble.

When thou liest down, thou shalt not be afraid: yea, thou shalt lie down, and thy sleep shall be sweet.

PROVERBS 3:23,24

And who is he that will harm you, if ye be followers of that which is good?

I PETER 3:13

Eternal Life

But God will redeem my soul from the power of the grave: for he shall receive me. Selah.

PSALM 49:15

For God so loved the world, that he gave his only begotten Son, that whosoever believeth in him should not perish, but have everlasting life.

He that believeth on the Son hath everlasting life: and he that believeth not the Son shall not see life; but the wrath of God abideth on him.

JOHN 3:16,36

Verily, verily, I say unto you, He that heareth my word, and believeth on him that sent me, hath everlasting life, and shall not come into condemnation; but is passed from death unto life.

JOHN 5:24

Then spake Jesus again unto them, saying, I am the light of the world: he that followeth me shall not walk in darkness, but shall have the light of life.

JOHN 8:12

My sheep hear my voice, and I know them, and they follow me:

JOHN 10:27

And I give unto them eternal life; and they shall never perish, neither shall any man pluck them out of my hand.

JOHN 10:28

Jesus said unto her, I am the resurrection, and the life: he that believeth in me, though he were dead, yet shall he live:

JOHN 11:25

And this is life eternal, that they might know thee the only true God, and Jesus Christ, whom thou has sent.

JOHN 17:3

For the wages of sin is death; but the gift of God is eternal life through Jesus Christ our Lord.

ROMANS 6:23

But if the Spirit of him that raised up Jesus from the dead dwell in you, he that raised up Christ from the dead shall also quicken your mortal bodies by his Spirit that dwelleth in you.

ROMANS 8:11

That if thou shalt confess with thy mouth the Lord Jesus, and shalt believe in thine heart that God hath raised him from the dead, thou shalt be saved.

ROMANS 10:9

Knowing that he which raised up the Lord Jesus shall raise up us also by Jesus, and shall present us with you.

II CORINTHIANS 4:14

For he that soweth to his flesh shall of the flesh reap corruption; but he that soweth to the Spirit shall of the Spirit reap life everlasting.

GALATIANS 6:8

For if we believe that Jesus died and rose again, even so them also which sleep in Jesus will God bring with him.

I THESSALONIANS 4:14

And this is the promise that he hath promised us, even eternal life.

I JOHN 2:25

And this is the record, that God hath given to us eternal life, and this life is in his Son.

I JOHN 5:11

And God shall wipe away all tears from their eyes; and there shall be no more death, neither sorrow, nor crying, neither shall there be any more pain: for the former things are passed away.

REVELATION 21:4

Food and Raiment

Trust in the Lord, and do good; so shalt thou dwell in the land, and verily thou shalt be fed.

PSALM 37:3

Blessed be the Lord, who daily loadeth us with benefits, even the God of our salvation, Selah.

PSALM 68:19

He causeth the grass to grow for the cattle, and herb for the service of man: that he may bring forth food out of the earth;

And wine that maketh glad the heart of man, an oil to make his face to shine, and bread which strengtheneth man's heart.

PSALMS 104:14,15

The people asked, and he brought quails, and satisfied them with the bread of heaven.

He opened the rock, and the waters gushed out; they ran in the dry places like a river.

For he remembered his holy promise, . . .

PSALMS 105:40,41,42

I will abundantly bless her provision: I will satisfy her poor with bread.

PSALMS 132:15

He maketh peace in thy borders, and filleth thee with the finest of the wheat.

PSALM 147:14

The righteous eateth to the satisfying of his soul: but the belly of the wicked shall want.

PROVERBS 13:25

And ye shall eat in plenty, and be satisfied, . . .

JOEL 2:26

Therefore I say unto you, Take no thought for your life, what ye shall eat, or what ye shall drink; nor yet for your body, what ye shall put on. Is not the life more than meat, and the body than raiment?

Behold the fowls of the air: for they sow not, neither do they reap, nor gather into barns; yet your heavenly Father feedeth them. Are ye not much better than they?

Wherefore, if God so clothe the grass of the field, which today is, and to-morrow is cast into the oven, shall he not much more clothe you, O ye of little faith?

(For after all these things do the Gentiles seek:) for your heavenly Father knoweth that ye have need of all these things.

MATTHEW 6:25,26,30,32

Heavenly Rewards

As for me, I will behold thy face in righteousenss: I shall be satisfied, when I awake, with thy likeness.

PSALM 17:15

For the Son of man shall come in the glory of his Father with his angels; and then he shall reward every man according to his works.

MATTHEW 16:27

His lord said unto him, Well done, good and faithful servant; thou hast been faithful over a few things, I will make thee ruler over many things: enter thou into the joy of thy lord.

MATTHEW 25:23

And I appoint unto you a kingdom, as my Father hath appointed unto me;

That ye may eat and drink at my table in my kingdom, . . .

LUKE 22:29,30

Henceforth there is laid up for me a crown of righteousness, which the Lord, the righteous judge, shall give me at that day: and not to me only, but unto all them also that love his appearing.

II TIMOTHY 4:8

. . . and so shall we ever be with the Lord.

I THESSALONIANS 4:17

To an inheritance incorruptible, and undefiled, and that fadeth not away, reserved in heaven for you,

I PETER 1:4

And when the chief Shepherd shall appear, ye shall receive a crown of glory that fadeth not away.

I PETER 5:4

He that overcometh shall inherit all things; and I will be his God, and he shall be my son.

REVELATION 21:7

And, behold, I come quickly; and my reward is with me, to give every man according as his work shall be.

Blessed are they that do his commandments, that they may have right to the tree of life, and may enter in through the gates into the city.

REVELATION 22:12,14

Peace

And I will give peace in the land, and ye shall lie down, and none shall make you afraid: and I will rid evil beasts out of the land, neither shall the sword go through your land.

LEVITICUS 26:6

I will both lay me down in peace, and sleep: for thou, Lord, only makest me dwell in safety.

PSALM 4:8

The Lord will give strength unto his people; the Lord will bless his people with peace.

PSALM 29:11

Mark the perfect man, and behold the upright: for the end of that man is peace.

PSALM 37:37

Great peace have they which love thy law: and nothing shall offend them.

PSALM 119:165

He maketh peace in thy borders, . . .

PSALM 147:14

Thou wilt keep him in perfect peace, whose mind is stayed on thee: because he trusteth in thee.

Lord, thou wilt ordain peace for us: for thou also hast wrought all our works in us.

ISAIAH 26:3,12

And my people shall dwell in a peaceable habitation, and in sure dwellings, and in quiet resting places;

ISAIAH 32:18

Peace I leave with you, my peace I give unto you: not as the world giveth, give I unto you. Let not your heart be troubled, neither let it be afraid.

JOHN 14:27

Therefore being justified by faith, we have peace with God through our Lord Jesus Christ:

ROMANS 5:1

And the peace of God, which passeth all understanding, shall keep your hearts and minds through Christ Jesus.

PHILIPPIANS 4:7

And let the peace of God rule in your hearts, to the which also ye are called in one body; and be ye thankful.

COLOSSIANS 3:15

His Second Coming

For I know that my redeemer liveth, and that
he shall stand at the latter day upon the earth:

JOB 19:25

. . . and they shall see the Son of man coming
in the clouds of heaven with power and great
glory.

Watch therefore: for ye know not what hour
your Lord doth come.

MATTHEW 24:30,42

When the Son of man shall come in his glory,
and all the holy angels with him, then shall he
sit upon the throne of his glory:

MATTHEW 25:31

And if I go and prepare a place for you, I will
come again, and receive you unto myself; that
where I am, there ye may be also.

Ye have heard how I said unto you, I go away,
and come again unto you. . . .

JOHN 14:3,28

. . . this same Jesus, which is taken up from
you into heaven, shall so come in like manner
as ye have seen him go into heaven.

ACTS 1:11

. . . waiting for the coming of our Lord Jesus Christ:

Who shall also confirm you unto the end, that ye may be blameless in the day of our Lord Jesus Christ.

I CORINTHIANS 1:7,8

Therefore judge nothing before the time, until the Lord come, who both will bring to light the hidden things of darkness, and will make manifest the counsels of the hearts . . .

I CORINTHIANS 4:5

For as often as ye eat this bread, and drink this cup, ye do shew the Lord's death till he come.

I CORINTHIANS 11:26

When Christ, who is our life, shall appear, then shall ye also appear with him in glory.

COLOSSIANS 3:4

And to wait for his Son from heaven, whom he raised from the dead, even Jesus, . . .

I THESSALONIANS 1:10

For the Lord himself shall descend from heaven with a shout, with the voice of the archangel, and with the trump of God: and the dead in Christ shall rise first:

I THESSALONIANS 4:16

Then we which are alive and remain shall be caught up together with them in the clouds, to meet the Lord in the air: and so shall we ever be with the Lord.

I THESSALONIANS 4:17

Looking for that blessed hope, and the glorious appearing of the great God and our Saviour Jesus Christ;

TITUS 2:13

So Christ was once offered to bear the sins of many; and unto them that look for him shall he appear the second time without sin unto salvation.

HEBREWS 9:28

And when the chief Shepherd shall appear, ye shall receive a crown of glory that fadeth not away.

I PETER 5:4

. . . but we know that, when he shall appear, we shall be like him; for we shall see him as he is.

I JOHN 3:2

Behold, he cometh with clouds; and every eye shall see him, and they also which pierced him: . . .

REVELATION 1:7

THE
BELIEVER IS . . .

Forgiven

To him give all the prophets witness, that through his name whosoever believeth in him shall receive remission of sins.

ACTS 10:43

In whom we have redemption through his blood, the forgiveness of sins, according to the riches of his grace;

EPHESIANS 1:7

Justified

And by him all that believe are justified from all things, . . .

ACTS 13:39

Being justified freely by his grace through the redemption that is in Christ Jesus:

Therefore we conclude that a man is justified by faith without the deeds of the law.

ROMANS 3:24,28

That being justified by his grace, we should be made heirs according to the hope of eternal life.

TITUS 3:7

A New Creation

Therefore if any man be in Christ, he is a new creature: old things are passed away; behold, all things are become new.

II CORINTHIANS 5:17

Sanctified

But of him are ye in Christ Jesus, who of God is made unto us wisdom, and righteousness, and sanctification, and redemption:

I CORINTHIANS 1:30

And such were some of you: but ye are washed, but ye are sanctified, but ye are justified in the name of the Lord Jesus, and by the Spirit of our God.

I CORINTHIANS 6:11

If a man therefore purge himself from these, he shall be a vessel unto honour, sanctified, and meet for the master's use, and prepared unto every good work.

II TIMOTHY 2:21

By the which will we are sanctified through the offering of the body of Jesus Christ once for all.

HEBREWS 10:10

Delivered From Condemnation

Verily, verily, I say unto you, He that heareth my word, and believeth on him that sent me, hath everlasting life, and shall not come into condemnation; but is passed from death unto life.

JOHN 5:24

There is therefore now no condemnation to them which are in Christ Jesus, who walk not after the flesh, but after the Spirit.

ROMANS 8:1

Sealed By The Holy Spirit

Now he which stablisheth us with you in Christ, and hath appointed us, is God;

Who hath also sealed us, and given the earnest of the Spirit in our hearts.

II CORINTHIANS 1:21,22

In whom ye also trusted, after that ye heard the word of truth, the gospel of your salvation: in whom also after that ye believed, ye were sealed with that holy Spirit of promise,

EPHESIANS 1:13

And grieve not the holy Spirit of God, whereby ye are sealed unto the day of redemption.

EPHESIANS 4:30

Made An Heir Of God

And if ye be Christ's, then are ye Abraham's seed, and heirs according to the promise.

GALATIANS 3:29

Wherefore thou art no more a servant, but a son; and if a son, then an heir of God through Christ.

GALATIANS 4:7

That being justified by his grace, we should be made heirs according to the hope of eternal life.

TITUS 3:7

Delivered From This World

Who gave himself for our sins, that he might deliver us from this present evil world, according to the will of God and our Father:

GALATIANS 1:4

Who hath delivered us from the power of darkness, and hath translated us into the kingdom of his dear Son:

COLOSSIANS 1:13

Blest With Spiritual Blessings

A faithful man shall abound with blessings: . . .

PROVERBS 28:20

Blessed be the God and Father of our Lord Jesus Christ, who hath blessed us with all spiritual blessings in heavenly places in Christ:

EPHESIANS 1:3

The Temple Of The Holy Spirit

Know ye not that ye are the temple of God, and that the Spirit of God dwelleth in you?

If any man defile the temple of God, him shall God destroy; for the temple of God is holy, which temple ye are.

I CORINTHIANS 3:16,17

What? know ye not that your body is the temple of the Holy Ghost which is in you, which ye have of God, and ye are not your own?

For ye are bought with a price: therefore glorify God in your body, and in your spirit, which are God's.

I CORINTHIANS 6:19,20

GOD'S GREAT
COMMISSION . . .

Go Ye

Go ye therefore, and teach all nations, baptizing them in the name of the Father, and of the Son, and of the Holy Ghost:

Teaching them to observe all things whatsoever I have commanded you: and, lo, I am with you alway, even unto the end of the world. Amen.

MATTHEW 28:19,20

And he said unto them, Go ye into all the world, and preach the gospel to every creature.

MARK 16:15

And said unto them, Thus it is written, and thus it behoved Christ to suffer, and to rise from the dead the third day:

And that repentance and remission of sins should be preached in his name among all nations, beginning at Jerusalem.

LUKE 24:46,47

Then said Jesus to them again, Peace be unto you: as my Father hath sent me, even so send I you.

JOHN 20:21

But ye shall receive power, after that the Holy Ghost is come upon you: and ye shall be witnesses unto me both in Jerusalem, and in all Judaea, and in Samaria, and unto the uttermost part of the earth.

ACTS 1:8

GOD'S GREAT SALVATION . . .

The Need

. . .The fathers shall not die for the children, neither shall the children die for the fathers, but every man shall die for his own sin.

II CHRONICLES 25:4

The wicked shall be turned into hell, and all the nations that forget God.

PSALM 9:17

Wherefore will ye plead with me? ye all have transgressed against me, saith the Lord.

JEREMIAH 2:29

The harvest is past, the summer is ended, and we are not saved.

JEREMIAH 8:20

The heart is deceitful above all things, and desperately wicked: who can know it?

JEREMIAH 17:9

Behold, I was shapen in iniquity, and in sin did my mother conceive me.

PSALM 51:5

What then? are we better than they? No, in no wise: for we have before proved both Jews and Gentiles, that they are all under sin;

As it is written, There is none righteous, no, not one:

ROMANS 3:9,10

— 179 —

They are all gone out of the way, they are together become unprofitable; there is none that doeth good, no, not one.

For all have sinned, and come short of the glory of God;

ROMANS 3:12,23

Wherefore, as by one man sin entered into the world, and death by sin; and so death passed upon all men, for that all have sinned:

ROMANS 5:12

Know ye not that the unrighteous shall not inherit the kingdom of God? . . .

I CORINTHIANS 6:9

How shall we escape, if we neglect so great salvation: . . .

HEBREWS 2:3

And as it is appointed unto men once to die, but after this the judgment:

HEBREWS 9:27

And whosoever was not found written in the book of life was cast into the lake of fire.

REVELATION 20:15

The Provision

But he was wounded for our transgressions, he was bruised for our iniquities: the chastisement of our peace was upon him; and with his stripes we are healed.

ISAIAH 53:5

. . . for he shall save his people from their sins.

MATTHEW 1:21

And ye will not come to me, that ye might have life.

JOHN 5:40

All that the Father giveth me shall come to me; and him that cometh to me I will in no wise cast out.

JOHN 6:37

For the promise is unto you, and to your children, and to all that are afar off, even as many as the Lord our God shall call.

ACTS 2:39

To wit, that God was in Christ, reconciling the world unto himself, not imputing their trespasses unto them; and hath committed unto us the word of reconciliation.

II CORINTHIANS 5:19

Who gave himself for our sins, . . .

GALATIANS 1·4

In whom we have redemption through his blood, the forgiveness of sins, according to the riches of his grace;

EPHESIANS 1:7

In whom we have redemption through his blood, even the forgiveness of sins:

COLOSSIANS 1:14

Neither by the blood of goats and calves, but by his own blood he entered in once into the holy place, having obtained eternal redemption for us.

HEBREWS 9:12

In hope of eternal life, which God, that cannot lie, promised before the world began;

TITUS 1:2

For the grace of God that bringeth salvation hath appeared to all men,

TITUS 2:11

And he is the propitiation for our sins: and not for ours only, but also for the sins of the whole world.

I JOHN 2:2

And the Spirit and the bride say, Come. And let him that heareth say, Come. And let him that is athirst come. And whosoever will, let him take the water of life freely.

REVELATION 22:17

The Plan

Jesus answered and said unto him, Verily, verily, I say unto thee, Except a man be born again, he cannot see the kingdom of God.

JOHN 3:3

For all have sinned, and come short of the glory of God;

ROMANS 3:23

For the wages of sin is death; but the gift of God is eternal life through Jesus Christ our Lord.

ROMANS 6:23

But God commendeth his love toward us, in that, while we were yet sinners, Christ died for us.

ROMANS 5:8

For he hath made him to be sin for us, who knew no sin; that we might be made the righteousness of God in him.

II CORINTHIANS 5:21

For by grace are ye saved through faith; and that not of yourselves: it is the gift of God:

Not of works, lest any man should boast.

EPHESIANS 2:8,9

For God so loved the world, that he gave his only begotten Son, that whosoever believeth in him should not perish, but have everlasting life.

JOHN 3:16

That if thou shalt confess with thy mouth the Lord Jesus, and shalt believe in thine heart that God hath raised him from the dead, thou shalt be saved.

For with the heart man believeth unto righteousness; and with the mouth confession is made unto salvation.

ROMANS 10:9,10

For whosoever shall call upon the name of the Lord shall be saved.

ROMANS 10:13

But as many as received him, to them gave he power to become the sons of God, even to them that believe on his name:

JOHN 1:12

Not by works of righteousness which we have done, but according to his mercy he saved us, by the washing of regeneration, and renewing of the Holy Ghost;

TITUS 3:5

The Assurance

Behold, God is my salvation; I will trust, and not be afraid: for the Lord JEHOVAH is my strength and my song; he also is become my salvation.

ISAIAH 12:2

He that believeth on the Son hath everlasting life: and he that believeth not the Son shall not see life; but the wrath of God abideth on him.

JOHN 3:36

My sheep hear my voice, and I know them, and they follow me:

And I give unto them eternal life; and they shall never perish, neither shall any man pluck them out of my hand.

JOHN 10:27,28

Now ye are clean through the word which I have spoken unto you.

JOHN 15:3

There is therefore now no condemnation to them which are in Christ Jesus, who walk not after the flesh, but after the Spirit.

ROMANS 8:1

. . . for I know whom I have believed, and am persuaded that he is able to keep that which I have committed unto him against that day.

II TIMOTHY 1:12

For then must he often have suffered since the foundation of the world: but now once in the end of the world hath he appeared to put away sin by the sacrifice of himself.

HEBREWS 9:26

These things have I written unto you that believe on the name of the Son of God; that ye may know that ye have eternal life, and that ye may believe on the name of the Son of God.

I JOHN 5:13

The Evidence

He brought me up also out of an horrible pit, out of the miry clay, and set my feet upon a rock, and established my goings.

And he hath put a new song in my mouth, even praise unto our God: many shall see it, and fear, and shall trust in the Lord.

PSALM 40:2,3

And hope maketh not ashamed; because the love of God is shed abroad in our hearts by the Holy Ghost which is given unto us.

ROMANS 5:5

For as many as are led by the Spirit of God, they are the sons of God.

The Spirit itself beareth witness with our spirit, that we are the children of God:

ROMANS 8:14,16

But the natural man receiveth not the things of the Spirit of God: for they are foolishness unto him: neither can he know them, because they are spiritually discerned.

But he that is spiritual judgeth all things, yet he himself is judged of no man.

I CORINTHIANS 2:14,15

Therefore if any man be in Christ, he is a new creature: old things are passed away; behold, all things are become new.

II CORINTHIANS 5:17

And hereby we do know that we know him, if we keep his commandments.

He that saith, I know him, and keepeth not his commandments, is a liar, and the truth is not in him.

But whoso keepeth his word, in him verily is the love of God perfected: hereby know we that we are in him.

He that saith he abideth in him ought himself also so to walk, even as he walked.

But ye have an unction from the Holy One, and ye know all things.

But the anointing which ye have received of him abideth in you, and ye need not that any man teach you: but as the same anointing teacheth you of all things, and is truth, and is no lie, and even as it hath taught you, ye shall abide in him.

I JOHN 2:3-6,20,27

In this the children of God are manifest, and the children of the devil: whosoever doeth not righteousness is not of God, neither he that loveth not his brother.

I JOHN 3:10

CONCLUSION . . .

God Will Perform All His Promises

God is not a man, that he should lie; neither the son of man, that he should repent: hath he said, and shall he not do it? or hath he spoken, and shall he not make it good?

NUMBERS 23:19

Blessed be the Lord, that hath given rest unto his people Israel, according to all that he promised: there hath not failed one word of all his good promise, . . .

I KINGS 8:56

And they that know thy name will put their trust in thee: for thou, Lord, hast not forsaken them that seek thee.

PSALM 9:10

My covenant will I not break, nor alter the thing that is gone out of my lips.

PSALM 89:34

He hath remembered his covenant for ever, the word which he commanded to a thousand generations.

PSALM 105:8

For ever, O Lord, thy word is settled in heaven.
Thy faithfulness is unto all generations: . . .
Thy word is true from the beginning: and every one of thy righteous judgments endureth for ever.

PSALM 119:89,90,160

. . . thy counsels of old are faithfulness and truth.

ISAIAH 25:1

. . . yea, I have spoken it, I will also bring it to pass; I have purposed it, I will also do it.

ISAIAH 46:11

And being fully persuaded that, what he had promised, he was able also to perform.

ROMANS 4:21

For all the promises of God in him are yea, and in him Amen, unto the glory of God by us.

II CORINTHIANS 1:20

For bodily exercise profiteth little: but godliness is profitable unto all things, having promise of the life that now is, and of that which is to come.

I TIMOTHY 4:8

That ye be not slothful, but followers of them who through faith and patience inherit the promises.

HEBREWS 6:12

That by two immutable things, in which it was impossible for God to lie, we might have a strong consolation, who have fled for refuge to lay hold upon the hope set before us:

HEBREWS 6:18

Let us hold fast the profession of our faith without wavering; (for he is faithful that promised;)

HEBREWS 10:23

Whereby are given unto us exceeding great and precious promises: . . .

II PETER 1:4

The Lord is not slack concerning his promise, as some men count slackness; but is longsuffering to us-ward, . . .

Nevertheless we, according to his promise, look for new heavens and a new earth, wherein dwelleth righteousness.

II PETER 3:9,13

Blessed is the man that endureth temptation: for when he is tried, he shall receive the crown of life, which the Lord hath promised to them that love him.

JAMES 1:12

And this is the promise that he hath promised us, even eternal life.

I JOHN 2:25

WHERE TO TURN IN YOUR BIBLE . . .

References:

When Tempted . . . . James 1:12-15

When Growing Old . . . . Psalms 71

When Needing Guidance . . . . James 1:5-6

When In Sorrow . . . . John 14:1-3

When You Worry . . . . . Matthew 6:19-34

When You Travel . . . . Psalms 121

When Contemplating
Marriage . . . . Matthew 19:4-6

When You Are Sad . . . II Corinthians 1:3-11

When Far From God . . . . . Acts 17:22-30

When Faith Is Weak . . . . . . Hebrews 11

When Men Fail You . . . . Psalms 27

When You Have Sinned . . . . . Psalms 51

When Lonely Or Fearful . . . . . Psalms 23

When Sleep Fails You . . . . . Psalms 4:4-8

When You Need
Assurance . . . . I John 3:19-24

NOTES

NOTES

_____

_____

_____

_____

_____

_____

_____

_____

_____

_____

_____

_____

_____

_____

_____

_____

NOTES

THOUGHTS

_____

_____

_____

_____

_____

_____

_____

_____

_____

_____

_____

_____

_____

_____

_____

_____

_____

THOUGHTS

_____

_____

_____

_____

_____

_____

_____

_____

_____

_____

_____

_____

_____

_____

_____

_____

_____

PRAYER LIST

_____

_____

_____

_____

_____

_____

_____

_____

_____

_____

_____

_____

_____

_____

_____

_____

PRAYER LIST

_____
_____
_____
_____
_____
_____
_____
_____
_____
_____
_____
_____
_____
_____
_____
_____